T0195660

Secrets
Of
Skincare

An Unconventional Approach To Healthy Skin

AMY RAE SEDLAR

BALBOA.PRESS
A DIVISION OF HAY HOUSE

Balboa Press books may be ordered through booksellers or by contacting:

Balboa Press
A Division of Hay House
1663 Liberty Drive
Bloomington, IN 47403
www.balboapress.com
844-682-1282

Print information available on the last page.

ISBN: 978-1-9822-7361-3 (sc)
ISBN: 978-1-9822-7363-7 (hc)
ISBN: 978-1-9822-7362-0 (e)

Library of Congress Control Number: 2021917916

Balboa Press rev. date: 11/17/2021

CONTENTS

This book is dedicated to my patient, loving husband and my 4 beautiful daughters. Without you there would be no me!

To my Mother who taught me that when you are consistent and persistent you will persevere.

PREFACE

Most of us really want to have beautiful, healthy skin! Yet I see so many people struggling with skin problems. They innocently go from doctors to skin care professionals to anyone from whom they can get answers, only to be left with empty promises and empty wallets. The answers are so simple, yet they feel so complicated. Ours is a world increasingly filled with so much information that we just don't know who or what to believe anymore.

If you are reading this book, you may have skin issues and you are hoping to find some real solutions. For those of you dealing with a serious skin issue for the first time, it can be terrifying to be that person in front of the mirror. It breaks my heart to think of the suffering that people go through when their skin acts up and they can't find answers. They feel like they want to hide their faces or their bodies. I have held many people in my arms who were in tears because they had given up hope of ever having beautiful skin. It doesn't have to be that way, though.

You can have gorgeous, glowing skin at any age. Your skin is your largest living organ. It protects you from all the things from which you really do want to be protected. If we see our skin for what it really is and treat it like a living organ, things can heal it.

This book is about the truth—the truth about how your skin works, how it reacts to all the products you unknowingly smear and slather on it, the foods that heal or harm it, and all the other secrets I have learned over my career. I hope this book brings you the information you have been looking for to help you on your path to healthy, gorgeous skin.

Love,
Amy Rae

CHAPTER 1

Skin Wars

Maybe you're reading this book because you've been everywhere and tried everything you can to clear up your skin issues. Maybe you've spent hundreds, possibly thousands, of dollars on treatments and products, and your skin is still suffering from acne, aging, rashes, rosacea, melasma, hyperpigmentation, psoriasis, or whatever other skin-related issues that so many people face today. Why, when we have more information and more technology than ever, aren't people finding answers and relief for their largest organ, the skin? In my career as an aesthetician, I have helped many people who were ready to give up and throw in the towel; some were even suicidal from the pain and suffering that comes with problematic skin. I have held people in my arms who were crying from the frustration of years of trying to figure out why their skin won't heal. I offered a new hope and a new approach to skin care, and it worked!

Being an aesthetician in Los Angeles for many years, I have worked on lots people who had to have flawless skin. Actors, models, and high-profile clients led me to become a perfectionist when it came to treating my clients' faces. I was determined to not just give temporary fixes but long-term results. It only made sense to look at the root causes of skin disorders to help my clients finally find the answers to the skin issues they were facing. Beautiful skin is more than just vanity; it is a reflection of what is happening on the inside with our health.

We desire healthy, glowing skin with no wrinkles, no acne, no pigmentation, and no red, ruddy complexions. We want beautiful, healthy skin because it is a symbol of youth, vitality, and health. Some people will do anything to get great skin. They will peel it, burn it, laser it, scrub it, needle it, inject it—the list goes on for days.

I'm not saying that some of these things do not work, but I can tell you from experience that *none* of these things will work long-term if you do not have a healthy body. The body is one system with many modalities. When I hear from clients who are shocked that food, nutrition, or lifestyle have anything to do with skin, I'm always baffled.

I'm sure there are many mornings when you wake up and look in the mirror, and there is just no way that the reflection is you. You did not look like that yesterday! You're puffy, your skin tone looks uneven, and you don't look your best. How could your skin look that different in one day?

Then you realize that you ate a ton of sugar, gluten, and fat the day before. You had a few glasses of wine, and you were super-stressed out.

That's all it takes to fatigue your skin. What is happening is that your body's largest organs are working hard to get rid of all the toxins you accumulated from the food you ate, the hormones you produced from the stress, and the wine you drank. Not only that, but before bed, you slathered chemical-laden creams all over your face and neck, thinking you were doing a good thing for your skin. In truth, the cream put an even heavier toxic load on your body's main detox organs—your skin, liver, and kidneys.

Now, imagine day after day and year after year in this type of lifestyle. Is it starting to click that this is a vicious cycle in which millions of people are spinning around, day after day after day? Then, when they have no improvement in their skin, they are left frustrated and confused. The three-hundred-dollar cream they are using doesn't seem to be working. Let's give it a *break*! Literally, let's give our skin a break.

Our organs are overworked, and they can't fight off the daily stressors when they are on overload from all the extra stressors we add. These stressors also affect our lives in many other ways besides our skin. We are up against what we put in our bodies and what we put on our skin intentionally, on top of the involuntary daily toxic burdens of everyday life.

Most of us do not have a lot of time to worry about what's in our food and body products. We just trust words like *natural, holistic,* and *preservative-free*. It's a full-time job to search and read labels to find foods and products that we can truly trust. If you take the time to get to know the brands and companies who are honest and have your well-being in mind, you not only support good people, but you get a product you can trust to put on or in yourself and your family.

This book offers an unconventional way to look at skin health. It's about going back to the basics of what works for skin heath. It's about taking a look at what we automatically trust as the truth and questioning things we have been taught. I question all things and prove them to myself before I trust them; I have been that way since I was little. I have tried to put all the things together in this book that have proven to give relief and results to my clients for many years. Some things may actually shock you and may seem like the opposite of what you currently believe. These secrets of my nearly twenty years of skin care come from seeing what actually works on clients and using these beliefs, time after time, with incredible results. We are up against more than what people realize when it comes to invaders in our bodies. We have to protect ourselves from people looking to cash in on our trusting nature. Your three-hundred-dollar cream may be contributing to the toxic load you are carrying. Open the trash can, and throw it in there. That's probably where it belongs!

CHAPTER 2

Clean Products

Having an at-home skin-care routine is important for maintaining gorgeous skin. One of the most important things in your home-care skin routine is that your products are clean and free of harmful chemicals. I cannot stress enough the importance of clean, nontoxic skin- and body-care products. Every product you put in contact with your skin is absorbed into the bloodstream and filtered by the detox organs. So when it comes to what you are putting on your body topically, the cleaner the better.

I have worn many hats in my twenty years in skin care. I was in the medical-aesthetic industry for the first thirteen years of my career. I worked with some of the top medical-aesthetic doctors in the nation. I got into arguments with some of them about chemicals administered topically on the skin.

I always had a strong intuition that the ingredients and chemicals used in the medical-grade skin-care products were doing more harm than good. Although you may see an immediate result from some of these kinds of products, I couldn't understand how the ingredients that were so toxic—and some of them cancer-causing—could have a beneficial impact on the client's skin, topically.

It only made sense to me that the long-term effects of these topical products were actually going to age the client, as well as put a heavy load on the detox organs; it was common sense to me. Still, year after year since then, I have watched countless toxic skin-care products come on the market, and people willingly buy them, with the belief and hope that the products will make them look younger and more beautiful. They slather on these expensive creams and truly believe they are working.

I became obsessed with making sure my clients, as well as my kids and I, used only organic, non-GMO products. My motto became, "If you can't eat it, do not put it on your largest organ." I was ridiculed by family, friends, and especially the doctors with whom I had worked; they said I was being crazy.

The really cool thing is now, after many years, I am not the only person who has started to question the ingredients in our topical products. Many new holistic, organic skin-care products have flooded the market, and some of them are wonderful. It is always a heartbreaker to me when a new product comes out, and it might be 95 percent clean, but the last 5 percent is toxic. Even if you're exposed to that little 5 percent of toxic chemicals day after day and night after night, eventually, the load adds up. And that's just from your face products.

Imagine when you add the air, water, and food problems we are facing on top of it. There are things that we just can't control in this world and that we have to accept. However, there are things we *can* control. There are opportunities in life in which we do have a choice, and we should take them seriously. Do the research and take the time to know how you are smothering your skin. It's so important to find products that are 100 percent clean, organic, and safe; products that are beneficial, not detrimental, to your health and skin. Remember, this means anything that you put on your skin, not just facial creams but deodorants, shampoos, makeup, body lotions, perfumes, and any other topical products. Also, beware of things you are breathing, like synthetic fragrances and perfumes. Watch out for new clothing that has a "funny" smell; this can be caused by fungicides, which are dangerous to our health as well. Wash your new clothes a few times before wearing, especially if you smell a strange odor.

It sounds like a lot to worry about, but it isn't. You can weed out 90 percent of the products on the market and find the ones you can trust. Those become your new go-to, and life becomes simpler. What's great is that on top of using clean products for you and your family, you are supporting people who care about you, your health, animals, and our environment. It's a win/win.

CHAPTER 3

Ingredients to Avoid

There are so many toxic chemicals out there, but I will include a list of ingredients that you should avoid that are super-common in skin-care products. These could potentially impact your hormonal health and, in turn, end up causing more skin problems for you in the future. It's almost mind-blowing that these ingredients are allowed in our topical products, given what we know about their possibly detrimental side effects.

The epidemic of hormone and skin problems, as well as general health problems, is only growing, not to mention that these chemicals contribute to the toxicity of the blood and actually age and dehydrate the skin. All the while you are smothering your largest organ in chemical-laden products, you are causing long-term skin-care damage, among other health problems, such as hormone disruption, toxic blood, thyroid dysfunction, infertility—and the list goes on. This includes hand soaps, dishwashing soaps, laundry detergent, and many other products that come in contact with your skin on a daily basis.

As I mentioned before, try to stay clear of things you breathe in as well, like air fresheners, fabric fresheners, car fresheners, and things you spray in the air. They contain artificial fragrance that may be potentially harmful to your health. I always cringe when I'm in a public restroom, and the little air freshener sprays automatically. I think, *Well, there is the poison spray. Run out of the bathroom fast, kids!* I like to breathe clean air, not chemical air, in the bathroom. We get enough pollution as it is without purposely spraying poison into the air. Ugh!

Watch out for the following ingredients in your products:

Phthalates

You will notice this substance is in just about everything, once you start paying attention. Studies show that this substance resides in every human who has been tested for it—it's everywhere. This substance wreaks havoc on your reproductive system, has been linked to developmental disorders in children, and interrupts hormonal balance.

Phthalates are often listed and hidden as a fragrance or other misleading names. Make sure to not use products with "fragrance." Stick to natural, organic essential oils for yummy smells in your products. Often, the true fragrance is so divine that you won't miss out on anything except a synthetic smell and a load of toxins.

Triclosan

Triclosan is often used in antibacterial products. It kills bacteria, but it also kills your health. This substance interrupts hormonal balance and disrupts your thyroid function. This can make you feel sluggish and tired. Steer clear of this substance in your skin-care products.

Methylisothiazolinone

This product, also known as MIT, is found even in baby products. It is shown to be a neurotoxin. In studies, rats that were exposed to MIT for only a short time were shown to have brain-cell damage—not something I want to put on my family's skin.

Benzoyl Peroxide

It's commonly used to dry out pimples, but that's not all it dries out. It also dries out your skin! This stuff is toxic and has been linked to the growth of tumors.

Petroleum

Petroleum is in so many skin-care products. Everybody knows that vaseline is petroleum jelly, right? However, it is often hidden under a different name. Yes, this is the same substance that your motor oil is made from, and it is a known carcinogen (cancer-causing agent). Do I want carcinogens in my skin-care products? Watch for names like xylene, toluene, mineral oil, and liquid paraffin.

Parabens

Parabens are commonly used in the cosmetic industry, and they are in just about everything. The main problem with parabens is that they are a major hormone disruptor. They can act like the hormone estrogen in the body, disrupting both male and female reproductive systems, thus inhibiting proper function. Parabens can also affect fertility and birth outcomes.

BHA and BHT

BHA (butylated hydroxy anisole) and BHT (butylated hydroxytoluene) are antioxidant preservatives that are added to beauty products as well as foods. BHA is identified as a known carcinogen by the US National Toxicology Program. BHA is added to cosmetic products that contain fats, like lipstick and eyeshadow. Animals exposed to BHA developed liver damage, as well as thyroid and stomach problems.

BHT was not found to cause cancer but did cause many liver and kidney problems in animals. It is extremely sad that they tested it on animals, but it's the dirty truth.

Fragrance

A pleasant smell in your skin-care products is always great, but any synthetic fragrance can potentially be an irritant and not good for your lungs or your skin. Opt for naturally derived scents from flowers and herbal oils. Have you smelled nature lately? It smells fantastic! Anything labeled as a "fragrance" should be nontoxic. Remember that just because it says *natural* does not mean it is safe.

Why Is There Sometimes a Positive Result with
Chemically Toxic Skin-Care Products?

It's my opinion that if you notice a "wow factor" from using a skin-care product that has toxic chemicals, it most likely contains some type of plumper or exfoliator that can make the skin appear to react positively to the product *initially*.

The long-term damage, however, that the chemicals have on the liver and kidneys far outweighs the immediate benefit. In time, they will make your skin worse.

This happens because your liver and kidneys are your filters. They take on the toxic burden to help your body discard the lotion or potion you smothered your skin in. You're not actually nourishing the skin. That's why you will see marketing ads for skin-care products say, "This product may reduce the *appearance* of fine line and aging and wrinkles."

Imagine if you put nutrients on your skin—*skin food*, I like to call it. Imagine how beautiful and happy your skin and your other organs would be.

On top of that, you probably don't see a big difference when using these chemical-laden products. If you think about it, do you see lines and sagging skin disappear? Probably not. So why do we keep doing the unthinkable—blindly believe that these products are beneficial and innocently spend ridiculous amounts of money on them?

It's called marketing. A good brander and marketing firm can sell poop on a stick and tell people it's good for them, and sure enough, people will line up to buy it—never questioning, never researching what it is they are slathering all over their biggest beautiful organ.

These firms can wrap it up in a fancy package, fund their own trials, and voilà!

La Poop in a bottle just became the number-one top seller.

It's not that far off, folks.

CHAPTER 4

Hydration

Are You a Raisin or a Grape?

I love to compare a raisin that is all shriveled up to a grape that is full of living water.

The wrinkled skin of the raisin is exactly what happens to our skin when we are dehydrated. The skin of a grape is taut and firm, the way our skin should be when hydrated. Our skin really pays a price when we are deprived of clean water that is full of life. It loses elasticity and becomes weak and fragile. Our skin is our largest organ and the protector of our insides, yet somehow, we don't see our skin as a living organ. We surely do not treat our skin like it's a living organ.

When I think of one of the main reasons for skin problems or skin that lacks a gorgeous glow, I realize that it is chronic dehydration. It is like a silent epidemic that we see frequently in the beauty world. So many people are dehydrated but have no idea. They may drink water, but they are still dangerously dehydrated, and their looks and health innocently pay for it.

Sure, we have heard for years that we should drink lots of water, but we have missed out on some key factors when it comes to water. We need to get back to the water that nature intended for us to drink. Our appearance is the smallest worry when it comes to dehydration. Our skin is a clear indicator of our health. Our health is the most important thing, for sure, and we can use our skin as an indicator of what is happening inside, if we know what to look for.

What Is Chronic Dehydration and How Does It Affect My Skin?

For starters, when you are dehydrated, you look, well, dehydrated. Your skin doesn't look plump and taut. It looks crepey and saggy. Not everyone will have the same effect from dehydration in the body. Some people naturally have more oil in their skin, and their skin will not appear to be as dehydrated as someone with thinner, dry skin. However, that does not mean that, on a cellular level, their bodies and skin aren't suffering from dehydration. If you are blessed with super-sebaceous, thick skin, and you are dehydrated, it can cause you to have breakouts. Your skin may overproduce oil when its hydration levels are unbalanced. Your skin may appear to be hydrated when it's oily but infact it could be lacking hydration.

Remember that oily skin does not mean hydrated skin. When skin overproduces oil, it can be from a moisture imbalance and dehydration.

Another thing to consider is that when you are chronically dehydrated, your blood becomes thick. Your blood can become thick from toxins, chemicals, and pathogens that constantly bombard us on a daily basis. If we don't have proper hydration, the pathogens cannot be carried out of the body properly. We have to be extra-defensive with our lifestyles at this time because of what we are up against environmentally. So many skin issues can be addressed with proper hydration, but not many people are talking about it.

When I see clients with lots of spider veins and varicose veins, I know that can be the first indicator that they are chronically dehydrated. I have seen people reverse vascular problems with proper hydration and blood purification. These are not known causes in the mainstream health communities.

If we are dehydrated, nothing flows or works properly. The bad stuff cannot be carried out of the blood through the organs properly, and the blood becomes thick and stagnant. Our skin starts to droop and looks tired, and our veins become stretched and enlarged and start to leak blood. Chronic dehydration often is the reason for varicose veins. Then the heavy metals in the body (we all have them) can start to oxidize, and you start seeing brown spots and liver spots (see chapter 13 for further explanation). When we drink fresh, clean, living water regularly, the oceans, rivers, and lakes of the body start to flow properly again. My clients have reported seeing their age spots, broken capillaries, varicose veins, and wrinkles fade significantly when they figure out the proper way to hydrate the body. It's a true game-changer—or should I say, skin-changer.

Six Signs You May Be Dehydrated

1. Chronically chapped lips
2. Dry mouth and thirst
3. Not sweating
4. Constipation
5. Irritability
6. Dry, flaky skin
7. Dry eyes
8. Not urinating

All Water Is Not Created Equal

It's very important to understand that all water is not the same. Even though you may not feel thirsty, you could still be chronically dehydrated. If you drink coffee or alcohol or eat foods with large quantities of salt, then you may be dehydrated. Even if you drink only one cup of coffee or one glass of wine a day, you could be paying a price internally. (I talk about coffee and alcohol to a greater extent later in the book.) Even if you drink lots of water, that does not mean it actually hydrates you. Here's why.

The water we drink these days is dead. We often buy bottled water that has been in a reverse osmosis machine and is completely stripped of all its life. The electrolytes in water also are lost when you take out the bad stuff through reverse osmosis. Our organs rely on electrolytes to hold on to the water in our cells, and if there are zero electrolytes, then the water just passes right through our systems. Our blood then becomes thick and soupy, as I mentioned earlier. So the much-needed hydration to help the body rid itself of toxins is lost if we don't drink the water that nature intended for the human body to thrive.

If your water contains chlorine, fluoride, and toxic heavy metals, it actually can contribute to your dehydration. Most of the bottled water today does not hydrate you. If your water has the same pH as a soda, you may want to consider another water choice.

Investing in a natural water purifier is well worth it. Otherwise, stick to natural spring water with a natural pH. Stay clear of artificially alkalized waters. Make sure your water bottles are the safest possible choice when buying plastic.

Some other hydrating liquids for gorgeous skin are cucumber juice, apple juice, and coconut water. All are excellent skin-hydration liquids.

Our water choices are *so* important. Water is life, and it's the number-one thing to invest in, worry about, and be particular about when it comes to your health and skin.

Water Solutions

What do we do in a world full of plastic water bottles and metal water pipes? What is our best solution? We obviously can't go to the rivers and streams daily to collect our water (wouldn't that be amazing?). We need to figure out solutions that will work best for our lifestyles. We also need to truly understand why water is so important to our fundamental health, not only for our skin health but for our mental and physical health as well.

When we understand and study the role of water on the planet and in our bodies, we can see that water is a living substance. It is also a life-giving substance. It holds a vibration and is full of important minerals that we need. Water also has memory and holds on to information. It's more alive than we will ever understand. Water is life.

We can learn a lot from people like Dr. Masaru Emoto, who has explained that water is a living consciousness and can be alive or dead. I strongly recommend reading his book on water titled "Secret of Water". It may help you understand the importance of and power that water can have on our health and our skin. In his studies, Dr. Emoto found that negative vibrations (sound, in the form of hateful words) changes the molecular structure of water. I believe that is true of the water that makes up 75 percent of our bodies. If we are around negative words and information, it can directly affect our energy, vibration and the structure of the water in our bodies.

Unfortunately, not everyone has access to or can afford the kind of water we *should* be drinking. If you are lucky enough to afford a water-purification system, then, of course, that is the best option. The trick here is in choosing the right system for your home. I would stay away from reverse osmosis and artificial alkalizers, if possible. Artificial alkalizers use an electrical machine that splits the water molecule. It has been linked to heart troubles, and doctors are just now starting to talk about it. This topic could fill an entire other book; you can research the process, if you like. Just know it's not natural and not good for you, especially your heart. If you have no choice but to use reverse osmosis (RO), just make sure it filters out fluoride and chlorine, as well as other toxins, like pesticides. Fortunately, the RO systems are getting more advanced and are finding ways to restore the electrolytes in a more natural way.

Some systems act like nature. They filter your water in the same structure through which water flows freely in nature and bring the water to life again through this process. These systems also naturally alkalize your water. Basically, they mimic the water you may find in nature in the best possible way.

Unfortunately, these systems are not cheap, and not everyone has thousands of dollars to spend on a water system. If you do invest in one, though, it will save you money and time in the long run.

Another option is to find a water store nearby that offers naturally filtered water. The key is finding water that has not been artificially alkalized. If you stick with bottled water, make sure to get spring water, and stay away from alkalized waters, unless they are naturally alkalized. As I said, artificial alkalization has been known to cause heart problems, and it's just safer to stick to things that are natural or that at least mimic nature.

Check the source of your water, and do the research to ensure you're drinking the highest-quality living water you can possibly get your hands on.

One of the most profound ways you can hydrate is to drink good, clean water with lemon upon rising each morning. The lemon will bring your water back to life and is full of antioxidants and nutrients that naturally detox your liver and wake you up in the most natural way. Add one-quarter or one-half of a lemon to your water at all times, if possible, especially in RO water or distilled water.

If you don't want to give up coffee or other dehydrating foods, just make sure you drink extra water to ensure your hydration levels are balanced. For instance, for every eight-ounce cup of coffee, drink an extra sixteen ounces of lemon water.

Eating lots of fresh, organic fruits also can keep your hydration levels up. Fruit contains living water. Fruits like grapes, dragon fruit, and berries are super-hydrating for the skin.

How Much Water Should I Drink?

There is no exact measure of how much water you should drink. Everyone has a different lifestyle and body weight. If you are working in the sun and sweating more than normal, you obviously need to replenish that water loss. If you work out often, you may need more than someone who does not work out as often.

Drink water when you feel thirsty and listen to your body. However you choose to measure your water intake, make sure you are getting enough and that it is clean.

Just think: *Do I want to look like a raisin or a grape?*

Drink up, drink clean, and do the research on where your water comes from.

CHAPTER 5

The Liver/Skin Connection

The Truth about Your Liver

It's hard for some people to wrap their heads around how the body really works. I think this is mostly because we have been conditioned in Western culture to not be connected to our bodies. We have a pill to fix everything, instead of searching for root causes. The body is a system that works in perfect harmony—if we give that system the right tools and acknowledge the truth about what we were designed to put into our systems.

Truth means good food, clean water, and keeping our minds free of negative thoughts and stress. We eat things unconsciously, believing that what we put into our mouths will not affect our skin, health, and mood. One of the most fundamental things we can do for our health and our skin is to understand the power of our livers.

Our livers always struggle to keep us healthy from the time they are developed in our mothers' wombs. I learned from Anthony William, known as the Medical Medium, that our mothers may pass down toxic livers to us. It makes perfect sense. That's why you see babies with eczema or jaundice when all they eat is breast milk. It starts in the womb. We never think about our livers and how much they work to protect us from the world's toxicity. We can't see our livers, so we do not see if they are sluggish, fatty, full of toxins, and struggling. What we can see, however, is our skin, our largest organ. Our skin can be a clear indicator that we are in trouble with our liver health.

Chemically, mentally, and physically, we are attacked every day by our surroundings. For example, just stress alone releases hormones that our livers have to filter. I always say that we can't ask for things to get easier right now—we need to ask for more strength, as well as more knowledge and more understanding of what is going on internally. Things are not headed in a direction of becoming easier in the world, and more and more people are sick and suffering.

The truth is, most of us are living with livers that are so full of pathogens and toxins that they don't function at an optimal level. Our blood can become toxic when our livers are not clean. Our blood nourishes our skin cells, so if our livers are burdened and our blood becomes thick, it can have a negative effect on our skin and on our health in general.

Remember that our skin is a living organ and is one of our detox organs. If the liver is slowed down and not filtering properly, our skin can pay the price and look dull and tired.

Lifestyle, Diet, and the Liver

The bottom line is that if we clean up the liver, our skin improves. I've seen it happen over and over again in my career. It works every time. So how do we clean up our livers? How do we take the burden off our faithful organ? One of the best ways to help clean out the liver is to cut back on fats and proteins that slow the liver function and clog it up. The amount of fat most people consume is not healthy, and our livers are suffering. Imagine a sponge on which you pour oils and fats. The sponge starts to expand from the weight of the heavy, thick fats, and toxins and pathogens get trapped and cannot be flushed out properly. The rancid oils, fats, and pathogens feed the viruses that hide in our livers and other organs. The viral load we all carry gets bigger, and that's when other issues start to manifest in the body and skin. To clean out our livers, we need to add hydrating fruits and veggies to our diets, which flush out toxins and dissolve fats in the liver. We need to clean up the viral load we are carting around. Antiviral fruits and supplements can aid in the liver clean-up process.

Drinking a warm glass of lemon water, first thing in the morning after you wake up, can cleanse your body in a natural way. Lemons are kind of like an astringent to the liver. Cutting back on meat, if you are a meat eater, is one way to cut down on fat intake. If you are vegetarian or vegan, you still need to be extra careful to not eat too many nuts, grains, and seeds that are full of fat. Even good fats contribute to the overload in the liver. Your liver needs living fruits, living vegetables, and living water, to function properly. When your liver heals, it can work properly to heal your skin and clean up the body.

We know now that the liver is your best ally against invaders in the body, and this incredible organ bears such a heavy load. It's always at work to help keep the bad stuff from harming you. There are so many ways to clean up the liver. You should consult a functional health care professional, one who understands the truth about the human body and health, to help guide you on a liver-detox program. You do not want to mess around with unloading tons of toxins into the body's system by doing any random liver cleanse. Many people claim to understand nutrition and the body, but make sure you are working with someone who genuinely knows what he or she is talking about. Recently, many nutritionists have put their clients on a Keto diet, with high-fat intake, telling them that this is a way to heal. I assure you that a high-fat diet is not the way to beautiful skin. A low-fat intake, with lots of living, life-giving foods, will bring your skin back to life. If some people think bacon will make your skin glow more than an apple will, run from them! They know not what they are talking about.

Foods to Avoid at All Costs for Gorgeous Skin and a Clean Liver

- Canola oil (Canola is in everything—yuck!), vegetable oil, cottonseed oil
- Soy
- Gluten
- Corn
- Dairy
- Sugar
- Carrageenan
- "Natural flavors" (This is actually MSG. It is in everything—especially kids' snacks and even baby food—so be careful!)
- Pork (Pigs don't excrete toxins as quickly as other animals)
- Shellfish (They are bottom-feeders.)

- Fried foods
- Processed foods
- Eggs (They feed viruses. I know, it's a shame. I love eggs, but they feed the bugs more than anything you can eat.)
- Farmed fish
- "GMO" foods of all sorts

CHAPTER 6

Meat and Coffee

I put these two topics together in the same chapter because they are so controversial. They also may be two of the hardest things to give up or cut back on that cause an acidic environment in the gut. We may see meat and coffee differently when we look at them in a new light. When we see how they affect us on a deeper level, it may be easier to give them up or at least cut back on them. Here's my opinion on why meat and coffee may contribute to skin problems.

Coffee

Coffee is a big part of our culture. It's part of our history, and it has a nostalgic effect on people. The aroma of coffee in the morning perks up our senses and makes us crave a cup. The problem with coffee—and any other caffeine—is its addictiveness, dehydration, and the adrenal fatique that happens from frequent, longer-term use.

We start out having it once in a while, and before we know it, we are up to three cups a day. I started drinking coffee regularly in my thirties. A few of the nurses at the medical spa where I worked would go out around 3:00 p.m. and grab a Starbucks. I regret the day I said yes to a cup when they ran out for the daily dose. I remember it so well. I had never really drunk coffee in the afternoon, but I had been working really hard, and I was very tired, so that rush of energy I got from the coffee was amazing! I was hooked. The very next day, I joined the daily coffee runs.

Since I was drinking my coffee at 3:00 p.m., I began staying up later, and then I started using coffee in the morning to wake up. Little did I know that I was starting a ten-year journey of disrupting my sleep and my mood, and I was dehydrating my skin!

I was perfectly fine before I started the coffee, but I became addicted to a morning coffee, and a 3:00 p.m. pick-me-up coffee. The vicious cycle began. I'm now in my forties, and I only recently was able to stop drinking coffee. It was one of the hardest things I've had to do; it was hell, actually. I loved my coffee, but after giving it up, I felt better than I had in ten years. I only wish I had stopped sooner.

When it comes to coffee, we often don't talk about the adrenal burnout, the crash we get after a few hours, the moodiness, the stained teeth, the brittle bones, and the dehydrated skin. When our adrenals get burned out from the artificial rush of adrenaline that coffee gives us, we can damage them. We are not meant to run on artificially stimulated adrenaline all day. We burn ourselves out with coffee, and that's why we crash from it in the afternoon. It's the rubber-band effect. You stretch the rubber band way out and get a high, and then—*snap*—you crash and the rubber band bounces back but lower than where it started.

Our adrenals getting burned out is the main cause for skin discoloration, hyperpigmentation, and melasma. Our adrenals are precursors for other hormones that control our melanocytes and pigmentation. It's a chain reaction of damage that happens in the body when we burn out these little guys. Protect your adrenals and you will protect your skin tone and color too. You also will protect your nerves, and we know nerves cause stress, so again, you will only benefit from losing the coffee high every day. Staying calm and keeping your nervous system healthy can lower the release of stress hormones. It seems like people fly around, high on a coffee buzz, all day and crash out their nerves. If you can get off the coffee train, you will have more energy, better sleep, and less anxiety.

Now, if you are someone who refuses to give up coffee, then make sure you are drinking extra water. Adding coconut water to your diet, if you are a coffee drinker, can also be beneficial. Try to limit your intake to one cup a day as well. If you are a morning coffee drinker, then make sure to drink lemon water upon rising *before* you drink your coffee. Eliminating coffee altogether will improve your skin, sleep, and mood tremendously. If you are using celery juice (I talk about this later in this book), then make sure you do the celery juice first, wait thirty minutes, and then have the coffee. You likely will feel so energized from the celery juice that you won't even want the coffee—and there's no celery juice crash midday. You will feel amazing all day. Celery juice is a great way to stop drinking coffee. It replaces it and becomes a new ritual. It may take a few days to get used to the taste, but as the celery juice alkalizes, kills the bugs, and hydrates you, you will start to crave it.

Meat

Let's talk about the meat controversy. There are such extreme, radical views on eating meat. One side swears it is harmful to your body, and the other swears you can't be healthy without it. Some people eat *raw* meat and swear by it. What should we do, and who should we believe?

Here's how I personally feel about meat: clean meat, the way nature intended us to have it, is good for *some* of us, in very small amounts.

I do not believe, however, that eating large amounts of meat every day is beneficial to *anyone*, even if the theory that those with type O blood need to eat some meat is true. Eating large amounts of meat is harmful not only to our bodies—meat can be hard to digest—but especially to our planet. Animal agriculture is a dark secret that is not a popular news headline. Animals are treated horribly, and the effect of farming such a mass amount of livestock for profit leaves a huge global footprint.

I have chosen to cut out meat altogether for the time being. That's mainly due to the animal abuse taking place and the environmental catastrophe that we are creating. Those two points were enough to make me question my meat intake; never mind the negative health effects of consuming too much meat on my body. I also chose to support my two older daughters who have chosen to go vegan. I am so proud of them and want to support them morally.

Morally speaking, we know that cutting back on meat or giving it up altogether would be beneficial for the planet and animals, but how can it benefit our skin? We are living in a time that is very hard on bodies and skin. We have much to defend ourselves against. When we eat meat, we slow down the body's ability to cleanse all the harmful things we are up against. If you have a health issue or skin disorder, I would suggest you stay away from meat altogether. Although meat does not feed viruses, bacteria, or bugs in the body, it does clog up our systems and especially our livers, due to the high-fat content. Even chicken is high in fat—most people are unaware of that. In my opinion, someone with psoriasis or eczema should not be eating meat at all. Meat is acidic, high in fat, and hard to digest. I do know many vegans who are thriving on a plant-based diet and have amazing energy and an amazing glow, but if you're a vegan, you must be sure to supplement a B-12 vitamin that is effective.

B-12 is essential for us to be able to properly produce energy at the cellular level. If you are not a meat-eater, make sure you eat lots of dark leafy greens and take a B-12 supplement, as that is crucial for your health and skin. Make sure that a professional helps you with your nutrition intake if you have a B-12 deficiency and are planning to stop eating meat.

I suggest staying away from pork and shellfish altogether. Shellfish are bottom-feeders and cannot excrete toxins properly. Pork has a high-fat content and is hard on the liver. Pigs also have very few functional sweat glands, making all the waste they consume hard to clean out of their systems.

Above all, be conscious of what you eat and how it can affect more than your drooling taste buds. Some people believe that the fear and adrenaline released during the slaughtering of the meat is absorbed by our bodies when we consume it. It's more of a spiritual issue for some. There also are hormones, antibiotics, and other ways they pollute the animals. We have to rethink our current animal agriculture situation. If we stop supporting the evils, then we can make a difference. Imagine if we did choose to continue to eat meat, after learning of the way things really work, but we only supported organic, humane farmers. Imagine if all the people who choose to eat meat cut back to two or three times a week, instead of two or three times a day. That's a topic for another book, but I will say that if you are a big meat-eater, cut back, not just for the health of your skin but for the health of our planet.

If you are a vegetarian or vegan and it's working for you, that's wonderful! We are all different, and we should listen to our bodies. Just make sure you are getting the right nutrients from whatever diet you choose. You can test these levels through blood work. For some good references on how meat affects our health, search online for "the China Study." The China Study examined the link between meat consumption and chronic illness and disease. It's an in-depth look at the meat controversy. I also recommend all of Anthony William's books on healing. His information has helped so many people. I use his books like health bibles. His information helped my oldest daughter to heal her SIBO (small intestinal bacterial overgrowth) and Crohn's disease. I will forever be grateful to him. She is now a full vegan, thriving by eating a no-meat diet, and is free of chronic illness.

CHAPTER 7

Alcohol

Alcohol and Skin Health

Can I drink alcohol and still have beautiful skin?

This is a big question. I can't tell you how often I get asked this question. I know it is not an easy one if you enjoy drinking. I know how hard it is for some people to cut alcohol out of their lives completely. Alcohol is a part of almost every culture. Many people suffer from addiction or from drinking more than they should. I know this because many of my clients have struggled with alcohol and feel trapped. I used to love to have my wine after a long, stressful day. It wasn't until I saw alcohol for what it truly is—a poison—that I cut it out of my life completely.

I hear this so often: "I am too stressed to stop my nightly wine," or "I need it to help me sleep." The excuses for drinking are never-ending. I think if we understood how alcohol affects us and our looks, we would think twice about drinking it.

The billions of dollars spent on alcohol marketing are working quite well. Basically, we have been programmed since the day we were born that alcohol is a normal part of life. It is required to have fun at every event, even kids' birthday parties. Next time you watch TV, notice how alcohol is in almost every movie and TV show. People pour into happy hour nightly to escape reality. Some of those people don't have a problem; they have one drink, go home, and it's all fine.

But a lot of people don't stop with one, and they are in a vicious pattern that is destroying their tissue and skin. Alcohol eats away at your body's tissue and destroys your detox organs. Over time, someone who drinks a lot will look worn out—not to mention the terrible effects it has on our nervous systems and other organs, especially our faithful livers. I am so passionate about this topic because it's one of the main reasons I see so many young people, as well as older people, suffering with skin issues. It seems that everyone is drinking way more than they should, but not very many people are talking about it.

Why Your Skin Looks So Bad after Drinking

Alcohol dehydrates your brain and your body. It slows down the body's ability to filter the normal, everyday toxins because the body is so busy working overtime to eliminate the alcohol. This happens from the moment you start drinking! The second you take a drink, your body goes into a state of stress, trying to eliminate the alcohol. It is poison. Your body only wants what is best for you, and it identifies alcohol as an invader—because it is.

Remember that we have detox organs. Our kidneys, liver, and skin are our main detox organs. Our kidneys and liver get overly stressed from alcohol, and our cells become dehydrated. Our liver produces an enzyme to metabolize the alcohol, and that enzyme produces a by-product called *acetaldehyde*. This by-product is so toxic to your cells and tissue that it actually dehydrates and ages you.

The body's response to toxins is severe inflammation, and that's where you see red skin. The capillaries are dilated and can cause pustules and other inflammatory responses. My clients have to be honest with me as far as their drinking habits go, but I can read their faces like a book. They know they cannot have the flawless, clear skin they desire if they continue to drink heavily or even moderately.

(But remember—if you are someone who only has a drink a few times a year, this is not for you!)

Fun Fact: The word *alcohol* comes from an Arabic word *Al-kuhl*, meaning flesh- or body-eating spirit (that's why alcohol is called "spirits"). But that's exactly what alcohol does—it destroys our bodies from the inside out. It dehydrates and destroys living tissue. It causes stress and anxiety from the chemical imbalance it causes in the brain. Contrary to most beliefs that alcohol reduces stress and calms you down, it is quite the opposite. Alcohol attacks your central nervous system. It is a neurotoxin.

Over all, the main reason your skin is taxed so dramatically from alcohol goes back to the liver. A damaged, stagnant, overloaded liver equals damaged skin.

The other detrimental effect of alcohol is the dehydration we talked about earlier in the book. Alcohol completely dehydrates your cells. It takes seven to ten days for alcohol to leave your system, so if you drink once a week, you are never completely free of alcohol in your body.

If you are struggling with alcohol, I strongly recommend Annie Grace's book, *This Naked Mind*. She also has seminars and many resources to help you get a handle on your habits. It is a way to set yourself free, mentally, from the grips of the subconscious and social beliefs we have about alcohol. Her information can help you cut away the shackles that have had you trapped in the lie that alcohol is fun or that we need it to have fun. I love her philosophy and the idea that your alcohol habits are not something you have to live with for the rest of your life, and you can fight them. You gain freedom with this information. After reading her books, I truly saw alcohol in a different light.

Having a few drinks occasionally is not going to change your life that much. If you are someone who drinks one or two glasses responsibly and enjoys it, just remember to hydrate yourself extra the day after.

But if you are someone who really likes drinking, you may want to take a look at your patterns. If you want beautiful, flawless skin, alcohol is not what you should be drinking. Switch out the alcohol with a fresh-squeezed fruit juice that will hydrate and cleanse your organs. Your skin will thank you for it.

CHAPTER 8

Fruit

The Truth about Fruit

If you want gorgeous skin, *eat fruit*! I cannot stress enough how good fruit is for you and your skin. Fruit has gotten such a bad rap. First of all, yes, sugar is bad for you. Sugar causes all kinds of problems in the body. Fruit sugar, though, is not processed sugar. It is *not* the same.

Your body can really benefit from fruit if you eat it the right way. Fruit contains many nutrients and sugars (glucose) that our bodies actually need to survive. In fact, most fruits have a low to medium glycemic index, so they do not result in a major spike in blood sugar. Some fruits can help balance blood sugar.

The life-giving vitamins and minerals in fruit are wonderful for helping you achieve a healthy glow to your skin. They are also beneficial in fighting disease.

Did you know that many types of fruit are antiviral? Eating fresh fruit daily can help prevent a viral overload that many people are facing but don't even realize. Viruses can live in our organs and wreak havoc on our health. It is one of the biggest shames of a lifetime to eliminate fruit from your diet. Unfortunately, more and more people are adopting the belief that fruit has too much sugar and that fruit is harmful. It's absolutely absurd!

Fruit equals beautiful skin—period. The best way to see if that is true is to look at someone who didn't buy into the whole fruit-is-too-much-sugar nonsense.

For best results, eat your fruit on an empty stomach. Eat it first thing in the morning, or for a healthy snack in between meals, or a couple hours after dinner for dessert. The main thing is not to eat a big meal and add fruit on top of it. It should be eaten alone, and don't be afraid to eat a big serving of fruit, especially for breakfast.

Eat two mangoes for breakfast, or three bananas, or four oranges. Eat enough so that you feel full and satisfied. One of the main benefits of fruit is that it helps the liver clean out unwanted toxins. Morning is a great time to eat your fruit because your body has been repairing itself all night while you were sleeping. When you wake up, morning is the time when your body wants to eliminate all the waste it was working on cleaning up overnight. It's like the cleaning crew is waiting by the back door to take out the trash. If you give your body fresh fruit and water in the morning, it will help the body flush out the waste, all while helping hydrate you and restoring nutrients.

Fruit is full of enzymes that help the digestive system break down food and pathogens. It is also full of living water that hydrates us. Chronic dehydration is a real problem for people, and we can improve hydration by adding life-giving fruits. The right serving of fruit can hydrate you better than water alone, due to the sugar, vitamins, and mineral content that helps with absorptions and electrolytes.

Most people are not aware that our brains need glucose to function properly. So many people are walking around with a glucose deficiency, suffering from moodiness and brain fog. You will not only start to glow and plump up your skin from adding more fruit to your diet, but you will notice your cognitive function improves as well.

Have you ever heard of someone having horrible skin from eating too much fruit? Most people who indulge in fruit have glowing, plump, healthy skin.

It's best to eat one type of fruit at a time. It allows the specific nutrients from that particular fruit to work on healing and hydrating the liver. Of course, you can eat different fruits together, but in my opinion, eating one fruit at a time is more beneficial.

And don't be afraid to eat more than one apple or mango at a time! Your skin will love you for it.

Top Fruits That Hydrate the Skin and Clean Out the Liver

- Watermelon
- Dragon fruit
- Cantaloupe
- Tomatoes
- Apples
- Strawberries
- Mango
- Grapes
- Kiwi
- Honeydew melon
- Blueberries (Wild blueberries are best; find them in your grocery's frozen-food section.)

CHAPTER 9

Veggies for Glowing Skin

Leafy Greens, Vegetables, and Skin

Just like fruits, vegetables contain lots of life-giving nutrients, minerals, and beneficial carbohydrates that your organs thrive on, including your skin. Vegetables also contain lots of enzymes that help your body break down proteins, fats, and carbs. They help clean out the liver, hydrate the body and skin, and give you the *glow*!

When you are healing from a skin disorder or problem, I recommend lots of leafy greens. Raw vegetables are the best option when you are trying to absorb the most nutrition. Once we cook our vegetables, they lose most of their nutritional value; that's why juicing has become so popular. You can juice large amounts of nutrients and drink them. The juice enters the bloodstream and delivers life-giving vitamins, enzymes, and other key nutrition that can help the liver function better to help keep our systems clean.

One of the main benefits from green veggies is the chlorophyll. Chlorophyll is like the blood of a plant, and it helps to detox, oxygenate, and build our blood. Clean blood equals a healthier liver and healthier skin.

The chlorophyll molecule is remarkably similar to human plasma. The difference is that it carries magnesium at the center, where human blood carries iron. These green gifts of nature help us rebuild and replenish our red blood cells. By eating them, you will increase energy and restore the glow in your skin.

There are so many varieties of vegetables, and trying out new recipes with vegetables is fun. Try looking into an organic farm delivery near you or a local farmers' market. Supporting our local farms is so important to keeping the quality of our living foods. Organic does matter; it is very important not to eat vegetables that have been sprayed with pesticides and other harmful chemicals.

Another thing you can do is collect wild edibles. Many different plants in the wild are edible. My daughters and I like to collect wild edibles and then juice them or throw them in a salad. They are nutritious and free! It is extremely important, however, that you know what you are eating; take a class on foraging, or read books or watch documentaries on the subject. It's a fun thing to do with your kids or partner, and it's also great to learn survival skills like these.

Most veggies are good for you, but below is a list of my top skin-healing vegetables—my favorites for skin health.

Cucumbers

Cucumbers are so hydrating and can help to cure chronic dehydration. They also fight acne, wrinkles, and rosacea due to their anti-inflammatory properties. Cucumbers are especially good for someone with kidney issues. Try to drink your cucumber juice alone, without anything else. Your body can use the hydration! Trust me.

Celery

Celery juice all on its own is so good for digestion and can help to heal the gut. It also cleans out the liver and colon. Celery juice has become a popular juice in the holistic health world and for good reason. It heals, and it works. The mineral salts from juicing celery on an empty stomach are most beneficial and have changed people's lives.

I recommend Anthony William's books if you are suffering from *any* illness, especially a digestive disorder. Anthony William was the first person to ever talk about celery juice and its amazing healing benefits. His information is like a health bible. I have seen miracles happen from following his information. Whether or not people think he is a quack, his information works. It deserves to be heard by people who are suffering. The best way to say if something is the truth or not is by the evidence. The evidence is clear when it comes to celery juice and its power to cleanse the body.

Spinach

Spinach is a great vegetable for skin health. Raw spinach is such a wonderful way to get our daily greens. Add a huge handful to your fruit smoothie, and you will not even know it's in there; it's almost tasteless when added to fruit smoothies.

Sweet Potato

Adding sweet potato to your diet can help digestion and skin problems, such as acne. All potatoes, in general, are very good for you, although sweet potato has more antioxidants and more vitamin A. They are healing and grounding.

Kale

Kale is a powerful leafy green with so many benefits. The nutrients in kale can help boost well-being. It contains fiber, antioxidants, calcium, vitamin K, and chlorophyll. It is also a good source of vitamin C and iron.

Of course, there are so many wonderful vegetables to enjoy. These are just a few of the vegetables that can benefit your skin health. Eating a rainbow of living foods is important to lift your life force and living vibration. It is vital to skin health and your overall well-being. Enjoy what God gave us to eat in its natural form, and your skin will be happy and healthy.

CHAPTER 10

DIY Skin-Care Products

Many new and wonderful organic skin-care lines are available. They are clean and safe to use. These brands are honest, transparent, and organic or wild-crafted. However, you can also mix your holistic ingredients at home to make your own skin-care products. Books and tutorials online offer information on how to make your own products. Here are some of my ideas for skin-care products that you might find in your pantry that will give you *long-term* benefits and nourish your skin.

Coconut Oil

Coconut oil is nature's gift to the skin. You can use it to remove makeup; oil cleanse with it; use it in masks; shave your legs with it; use it as a body lotion, a moisturizer, or an oil pull; for eyelash growth—and so much more.

After I wash my face, I love using coconut oil to do an oil cleanse. You simply wash and exfoliate; then take a small amount of coconut oil and massage it into the skin in a circular motion; and then wipe it clean with a cloth. Oil is a pulling agent and can get deep into the pores to remove any leftover dirt after the cleanse. On top of that, coconut oil is antibacterial and super-hydrating, and it calms inflammation. It even works on acne. Make sure it's organic and has no added ingredients.

Be careful with coconut oil, as it can be oily and messy. I like to use it after a bath at night, and then wait to let it absorb before getting into bed so the sheets do not get oily. It does stain, so be careful.

Other great oils for skin care are grapeseed oil, almond oil, and avocado oil.

Apple Cider Vinegar

Apple cider vinegar is a great toner. I don't recommend it for internal use, but topically, on the skin, it's wonderful! Dilute it with a little water, and it is an excellent skin brightener. It also works wonders on hyperpigmentation and age spots. It breaks down dead cells and also balances pH.

For sensitive skin: Mix 1 part apple cider vinegar with 4 parts water.
For normal/dry skin: Mix 1 part apple cider vinegar with 2 parts water.
For oily skin: Mix 1 part apple cider vinegar with 1 part water.

Baking Soda

For an exfoliator, you can use baking soda. It's a great scrub and also brightens your skin. Be careful that you do not leave the baking soda on your skin too long, as it can cause peeling. A spoonful with a little water— or even better, lemon juice—will help brighten and exfoliate your skin.

Walnut Shells, Salt, or Sugar

Other exfoliators are finely ground walnut shells, salt, or sugar—foods that are coarse and that will allow a safe, gentle exfoliation. You can add the grit to an oil base or just lather up your cleanser and add a teaspoon of the grit to it. Rub in a circular motion. Make sure to include neck, chest, and arms if you want smooth skin.

Bentonite Clay Mask

If you have a powder form of bentonite, you can use it as a mask. It is wonderful for unclogging pores and delivers a nice dose of minerals and nutrients to the skin at the same time. It is the epitome of a detox mask.

Fruit Mask

These masks are great for brightening and plumping up the skin. It's a gentle way to exfoliate. You can use different fruits that contain enzymes to make lovely masks from them. Some of my favorites are pineapple, papaya, mango, and blueberries. You can add a touch of honey for an extra boost of hydration to any mask.

Fruit Mask Recipe (for dry skin, dull skin, acne, and pigmentation)

1/4 papaya
2 large strawberries
1/2 tablespoon honey

Mix and mash together the fruit and honey. Apply a thin layer to the face, neck, and chest. Do not leave on this mask for more than twenty minutes. If redness or stinging occurs, remove immediately. It is normal to feel a slight tingle.

Green Mask

Many nutrients are found in green plant life. Making a mask from dark leafy greens like kale and spinach can be amazing for your skin. Blend a handful of greens, and add a little spirulina powder or a green powder of your choice—organic, of course. Mix in a little of your bentonite clay if you are more oily or perhaps a little aloe vera gel if you are on the dry side.

Green Clay Mask Recipe (for aging or dull skin)

1 handful spinach or kale
1 tablespoon bentonite clay powder

2 tablespoons aloe vera gel

1 tablespoon clean water

1 tablespoon spirulina, wheat grass, or other green powder (organic)

Mix well, and apply a generous layer to the face and neck. Leave on as long as you want—the longer the better, at least twenty minutes. Store any leftover in a glass jar in the refrigerator for up to one week.

Castor Oil

I could go on and on about castor oil. Castor oil is incredible, but it's rarely talked about in the mainstream beauty world. Most people think of castor oil as being from the old days. I'm here to tell you that castor oil is one of the best beauty products you will own, not to mention that it's inexpensive, sustainable, and free of toxic chemicals.

There are so many uses for this simple oil. One of the most amazing and overlooked benefits is the ability to get rid of age spots. It can erase skin growths such as warts, moles, skin tags, keratosis, liver spots, and even superficial hyperpigmentation.

It has antiviral, antimicrobial, and antibacterial properties and can be used on acne. It plumps up wrinkles and fades scars like magic. I used it on all of my C-section scars (along with honey and silicone strips), and it worked wonders. Another amazing benefit of castor oil is its ability to help your lashes and eyebrows regrow. If you are like the many women who have over-tweezed and have thinning brows, rub a bit of castor oil every night on a clean brow, and watch the growth begin. Some other benefits are its wound-healing, antifungal, and anti-inflammatory properties.

If you apply castor oil to a sore muscle, it can reduce inflammation and help the muscle heal. Be patient; it doesn't happen overnight. You will need to give the skin a few weeks before you'll see significant changes. You will see, however, immediate hydration and plumping.

You can also do castor oil packs. Below, I have given instructions on how to make a castor oil pack. These can be used anywhere on the body. It's a wonderful thing to place over sore muscles or aching back, legs, or arms and especially over the tummy area, where your liver and gallbladder are located.

These packs will help stimulate your liver and gallbladder as well as your lymphatic system. This means clearer, brighter, more beautiful skin. You can also place the packs on the face to help relieve puffy eyes and dry skin. I like to do a castor oil pack on my face often. It really helps plump up the skin if you're dry. Do it the night before an event, and you will notice how dewy and fresh your skin looks.

Castor Oil Pack

Materials for a castor oil pack:

- Three layers of undyed wool or cotton flannel (must use a natural fabric)
- Organic castor oil
- Plastic wrap
- Hot water bottle
- Container with a lid
- Old material you don't want anymore (castor oil will stain)

Directions for a castor oil pack:

1. Place the flannel in the container. Soak it in castor oil so that it is saturated but not dripping.
2. Place the pack on desired body part.
3. Cover with plastic wrap.
4. Place the hot water bottle over the pack. Leave it on for one hour. Relax while the pack is in place.
5. You can store the pack in the covered container in the refrigerator. Each pack may be reused up to fifteen times. Make sure that with every use, you apply it to very clean skin. Keep pack clean by using it only on clean skin and then storing in a sanitary container.

Colloidal Silver

Applied topically on the skin, colloidal silver can work wonders. It's basically nanoparticles of silver suspended in water. The benefits of pure silver have been recognized for ages. It has antibacterial and antifungal properties that make it a miracle serum for acne and cystic acne. I encourage you to find the root cause of your acne issues, but using a topical product like colloidal silver can aid in your skin-care solution journey for acne. It also helps to repair skin tissue, making it wonderful for aging and scarring.

You can find colloidal silver in a gel form; that is what I recommend for topical skin use. You can use it like a serum under your moisturizer. I don't recommend using colloidal silver internally.

Hydrosols

Hydrosols are a great way to get essential oils infused into the skin without being too harsh. Basically, hydrosols are essential oils diffused lightly into water. There is a process that you can do at home very easily with any one of your favorite herbs or plants. (You can find many tutorials readily online.)

It's a wonderful way to hydrate and tone and, as I like to say, to deliver the *soul of the plant* into the skin. You are capturing the essence of the herb or plant, and it can feel pleasant when you spray it on the skin.

Hydrosols are safe for babies and children as well. If you have never heard of hydrosols, they are worth taking a look at. I love them and use them every day as a toner. My personal favorite is frankincense. I feel the ancient wisdom in the plant, and with my dry skin, it really helps me stay hydrated. There is a wide array of hydrosols to choose from.

Vitamin C—Topically

There are many serums and potions that you can apply topically to the face, but I really love the benefits of vitamin C. It has such a wonderful, brightening effect, and I have seen it give many dull complexions back their glow!

I do believe that vitamin C, taken internally, can be more aggressive at potentially healing skin disorders and various other health issues. The best scenario is to use vitamin C both internally and topically.

As with *any* vitamin, it is essential to know the source of the vitamin. (I talk about this in the "Vitamin C—Internally" section of the book.)

Most vitamin C is derived from GMO corn or other sources that we don't want to support or use on our skin. Finding a topical vitamin C can be mind-boggling due to the thousands of skin-care products that have flooded the market. The great thing is that you can rule out about 90 percent of them right off the bat because they are synthetically processed.

These are the things to make sure of when finding a topical vitamin C:

- Is it stabilized?
- Is it organic and non-GMO (not derived from GMO corn)?
- Is it packaged in an amber bottle to avoid heat and sun?
- Is it animal-cruelty–free and vegan?
- Is the concentration of vitamin C at least 20 percent?

Lemons—Topically

One of my favorite natural beauty tricks for brightening skin tone is lemon. Lemon is a great way to even out skin tone over a long period. Lemons are full of vitamin C. They are also antibacterial, loaded with antioxidants, and can be used safely on the skin.

Simply squeeze a little lemon juice from a fresh-cut, organic lemon into your palm and pat it into your skin. You can use it on your face, neck, and chest. You can also use lemon on your arms and hands as a great way to keep sun spots evened out, if you are prone.

Lemon juice is not an overnight miracle fix. It is a trick you can use as part of your daily regime. It brightens, tightens, and tones your skin in a beautiful, natural way. I have a huge lemon tree in my backyard, and I pick a lemon every morning so it is fresh with living water and sun. I will use half in my water for the day and then divide the other half into my green juice and on my skin. A lemon a day keeps the sunspots away!

CHAPTER 11

Exfoliation and an At-Home Facial

I am a big believer in exfoliation. I exfoliate every single day. Many skin-care professionals disagree with me; they think it's too much abrasion, and it strips the skin of its natural oils and so forth. I disagree. A nice, light daily exfoliation for most skin types can be beneficial and keep skin bright and healthy.

I believe it is a secret weapon against fine lines and wrinkles. Your skin has many layers and is constantly renewing itself by cell turnover. Cell turnover starts to slow down as we age. It makes sense that if we help our cells turn over as they slow down, it is beneficial to the skin.

I love to use the *wound-response theory*. Whenever we wound our skin, we trigger new skin growth, and our skin goes into healing mode. It makes sense that exfoliation is a light wound and therefore would trigger a wound response of healing and new skin growth.

Sometimes when I'm out and about, I see certain people and would just love to get hold of them and scrub their skin! One exfoliation could take layers off and make such a difference. Some people have *never* exfoliated. It can make a huge difference when we shed old, flaky layers of skin. We look brighter, our products absorb more easily, and we trigger new growth.

If your skin is super-sensitive, a cleanser with an enzymatic property that exfoliates may be a good option for you. If you have found that a scrub irritates your skin, you would be the exception to daily exfoliation from a scrub. But if you don't have super-sensitive skin, exfoliation could change your skin.

This does not mean you should scrub your face raw every day; it means a light exfoliation daily. You can use a scrub that is gritty and coarse to lightly rub away old, dead skin cells. If you have open scabs or active acne, do not scrub over those areas. You don't want to risk scarring or creating more of a wound. But a light scrub will help your pores to stay clean and stop them from being clogged with old oil and dirt. Giving the skin a light stimulation every day wakes it up and reminds it you are taking care of it. Some scrubs just don't work and are a waste of money and time, so choose one with a nice grit.

Another great form of exfoliation is natural enzyme peels. Fruit peels are great because they contain enzymatic properties from the fruit that help to melt away old, dead skin. You can make homemade enzyme peels from fruit at home. I have listed some great recipes for at-home peels and masks in the "DIY Skin-Care Products" section of the book (chapter 10).

At-Home Facial

Here's how to give yourself a facial:
This is an opportunity for you to do a deeper exfoliation and clean out your skin to maintain skin health. Giving yourself a weekly facial at home is a great way to take care of your skin in between professional treatments.

Step 1: Cleanse

Choose an organic, nontoxic cleanser appropriate for your skin type. Thoroughly remove all the dirt and oils.

Step 2: Exfoliate

Exfoliate really well in this step. Take a homemade scrub or a Buf-Puf exfoliator and scrub in a circular motion, removing all the dead skin cells.

Please do not be afraid to really scrub and get a nice rosy glow. The only contraindication would be if you have open wounds or cuts from acne; in that case, scrub around that area. If you are super-inflamed, skip this step and do a fruit enzyme mask to remove any dead skin.

Step 3: Oil-Pull Cleanse

Choose an oil: coconut with a couple of drops of tea tree for acne works well, or coconut with a couple of drops of rosemary for acne or dry skin. Rose oil is also great for dry skin.

After exfoliation, wash off the scrub and apply oil in a circular motion all over the face, neck, and chest. Oil has a drawing effect so even though you already washed and scrubbed, you are using the oil to pull up any leftover residue from soaps and scrubs, as well as pulling any leftover dirt or sebum from the pores.

I like to use oils that are antiviral and antibacterial, such as coconut, and add a few drops of an essential oil, like rose or tea tree, depending on the type of skin you have. Adding this step to the facial is well worth it. Your skin will look clean and start to glow. You can wash off any extra oil after your oil-pull cleanse.

Step 4: Toner

Use a toner every time you wash your face. Why? Is it that important? Yes! With every cleanse you do, you strip your natural oils. A toner is a great way to restore your skin's natural pH.

There are many amazing toners you can buy, or you can make your own. Using a base of apple cider vinegar, rosewater, witch hazel, or an herbal tea and then adding essential oils or herbs is a great way to tone the face after a good cleanse and exfoliation.

Step 5: Moisturize

After you're cleansed, scrubbed, and toned, you will want to seal in some hydration. For a daytime application, you can use a lighter hydration, and at night, you can use something a little heavier, depending on your skin type. Below are some suggestions, based on skin type, for some natural, nighttime skin moisturizers.

Nighttime dry skin options from the kitchen: castor oil, coconut oil, shea butter

Nighttime oily skin options for acne and scarring: tamanu oil, coconut oil, raw honey

Another Word on Masks

I suggest using a mask that suits your skin type once or twice a week. If you have acne, do a detox mask or an antibacterial mask. If you are concerned about aging, a nutrient-rich mask with enzymes and hydration would suit you. If you are suffering from rosacea or inflamed skin, a calming, soothing, anti-inflammatory mask would be your go-to.

I have listed a few DIY masks in chapter 10 that you can safely use. There are also many amazing organic skin-care lines you can trust that are conscientious and clean. Again, just do your research and make sure you know what is in your products.

CHAPTER 12

Secret Treatments That Work

Mewing

Mewing is a facial reconstructing technique that is free, easy to learn and can improve the direction in which our facial structure ages, as well as correct existing facial bone structure. It has been proven to help your facial structure develop more attractively as you age. It is a way in which we hold our tongues and our jaws in a certain position constantly unless we are eating or talking. This in turn helps support the jaw and skull and insures that you are breathing properly through your nose. Mouth breathing has been linked to physical changes in the face of children and adults. One of the most common side effects of frequent mouth breathing is an elongated face. There have actually been experiments done on monkeys where they have sewn the nostrils shut and these subjects had facial distrotion such as the entire face caving in. Mewing helps ensure that we are breathing correctly, supporting our jaws and getting the much needed oxygen through the nasal passage.

Mewing was invented by Dr. Mew, a London Orthodontist whose father is renowned for inventing "orthotropics". Orthotropics is a holistic approach to orthodontics. Conventional orthodontics believes that poor facial development and crooked teeth is a result of genetics. Orthotropics believes that poor facial development and crooked teeth are a result of poor diet, poor posture of the tongue and jaw and improper breathing. I agree with Dr. Mew on this. The evidence was pretty clear to me when I see the before and afters of avid Mewers. I also noticed a tremendous difference in my own posture and jaw line from making mewing a part of my everyday life.

How to Mew

When I first started practing mewing it felt a little awkward. I had to constantly remind myself to shut my mouth and position my tongue properly. Here are step by step instructions to properly do this technique:

- First relax your mouth and tongue
- Keep your mouth closed and your teeth just barely resting in your natural bite
- Move your tongue to the roof of your mouth and make sure it is pressed flat along the entire area, especially the back of the tongue pulled up to the roof of the mouth. You will feel the under part of your chin tighten up. You will feel a tighter jaw from this.
- Make sure your nasal passage is free and open. Taking certain herbs can help if you have sinus congestion.

Use this technique whenever possible. If you make this a habit, it will become a natural position for your tongue and jaw to be in. There are many resourses and information on Mewing. Do your own research and make sure you are doing the technique properly.

Facemapping

Facemapping has been used in Chinese medicine and ayurvedic practice for centuries. It is the belief that your face can be a map to the rest of your body's organs and state of health.

I used facemapping with my clients because it proved accurate most of the time. I know that using it on myself also has proven accurate. It's a really cool tool you can use to determine if something is going wrong inside your body. Below, I have included the face map that I have found to be the most useful and accurate in my career to help my clients' skin look its absolute best.

Pay attention not only to breakouts but also to broken capillaries, redness, and age spots. When they appear on certain areas of the face, your skin may be trying to tell you something. You can also tell a lot by the type of breakouts or blemishes you have in certain areas. For instance, if you are getting cystic type acne, that could be a sign of hormonal imbalance or a blocked-up liver.

See the face map below:

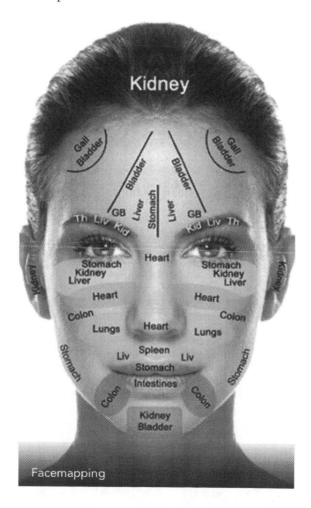

Facemapping

Sauna

One of the greatest tools you can use to help detox your skin is a sauna. My favorite type of sauna is an infrared sauna. One main difference between a traditional sauna and an infrared sauna is how hot the air in the unit becomes.

A dry sauna can use temperatures as high as 180 to 190 degrees Fahrenheit or more, which can be too hot for those who are sensitive to high heat. Infrared saunas use a much lower temperature of between 115 and 155 degrees Fahrenheit. The benefit of using an infrared sauna versus a traditional dry sauna is that you can achieve a deeper sweat at a lower heat. The infrared heats up the tissue and helps the body release toxins. A traditional sauna heats up the air—and your body gets hot and sweaty. Infrared saunas are easy to stay in comfortably for up to an hour, and you sweat an incredible amount without getting too hot.

It's very important to take water into the sauna with you and drink lots of it during the sweat-out. A recommended time is thirty minutes, but if you feel you are healthy enough and it feels right, you can go a little longer. I usually sauna for fifty to sixty minutes and try to drink one-half to a full gallon of water to replace all of the water loss from sweating.

The great thing about the sauna is that you come out feeling incredible. You feel lighter, clearer, and more alive. It gives your liver and other organs a break and aids in detoxing things like pesticides, heavy metals, and other things we are exposed to daily. It's also great for back pain and inflammation.

Hippocrates talks about a self-induced fever and how that is a sign the body is fighting an illness. Sweating is a way for the body to clean out. The body knows exactly how to heal itself, if we provide it with the right tools to do so.

The sauna is beneficial for most skin conditions such as acne, rosacea, psoriasis, eczema, aging, and melasma. I think that the sauna is so beneficial because it gives the liver such a well-needed break to help flush out some of the toxic burden the liver would otherwise have to deal with alone.

If you cannot afford a home sauna, many places offer infrared sauna sessions for a reasonable price. You will feel a difference after one sauna session—and then you will look and feel better with each session!

Sunlight

I am probably the only aesthetician who will ever tell you to get some *sun*!

Over the past twenty years or more, we have become afraid of the sun. It's a tragedy! Millions of people are smothering their skin with toxic sunscreen every day. Most sunscreens are laden with very toxic chemicals and are absolutely the last thing your poor skin needs to be smothered in daily. Remember that your skin is a living organ. It needs to be nourished and protected with things that actually protect it, not damage it.

Did you know that eating nutrient-rich foods full of antioxidants are actually a natural internal sunscreen? They protect your skin from the sun's harmful rays by providing antioxidants that neutralize free radicals—so your skin can soak up the nutrients from the sun. That is why some people who have had lots of sun exposure throughout their lives still have gorgeous skin. They had a diet that was full of life-giving nutrients, and the sun did not affect their skin in the same way as those who had less of a nutrient-rich diet.

Of course, skin type is the main factor of how the sun affects the skin. It is very important to be very careful with your individual skin type and never get a sunburn.

For instance, someone with a darker skin tone can handle more sun exposure and will take longer in the sun to absorb vitamin D than someone with a lighter skin tone.

The general rule that I tell my clients is this: cover your face, and let the sun hit an exposed part of your body for anywhere from five to thirty minutes. The lighter your skin, the less time in the sun. Look up your skin type on the Fitzpatrick scale, and make sure you're being safe with how much sun you get.

Adding sunlight to your life can make you feel better and look better. You'll have more energy, and it will boost your immune system. You will be happier from the increased level of serotonin. Low serotonin is a major contributor to the depression epidemic that this country faces. Sunlight will give you a daily dose of much-needed *natural* vitamin D.

Vitamin D is just one of the vitamins that the sun helps us absorb. We need sunlight just as plants and animals need sunlight. To deprive ourselves of this free energy that sits above us, patiently and graciously giving life, is just a shame!

The rules for sun, in my opinion, are to get a little each day that suits your skin type, but get *very* little—if any—on your face. Unless you work outdoors and are exposed to sunlight all day, skip the sunscreen, and save it for the times you really need it, like going to the beach or hiking. Small exposure to the sun, like walking in and out of your car to a store, is needed. If your diet is rich in life-giving nutrients and antioxidants, you need not worry about the damage. The damage comes from not eating right.

Soak up the sun, and be cautious of what works best for you. We are all different and have different skin types.

Where are you on the Fitzpatrick scale? The following list shows the six categories of the Fitzpatrick scale

Type I	always burns, never tans (palest; freckles)
Type II	usually burns, tans minimally
Type III	sometimes mild burn, tans uniformly
Type IV	burns minimally, always tans well (moderate brown)
Type V	very rarely burns, tans very easily (dark brown)
Type VI	never burns (deeply pigmented dark brown to darkest brown)

Dry Brushing, Lymph Drainage, and Skin

The lymphatic system is a complex system of tissue and organs, made up of lymph vessels, lymph nodes, and lymph that help your immune system and act as your body's drainage system. This lymphatic system is located just below your skin. It is constantly working hard to make sure the body is able to properly cleanse, detoxify, and maintain fluid levels. The primary function of this system is to transport the watery fluid called *lymph*, which contains white blood cells, throughout the body. These white blood cells are key to fighting infection and aid the body in expelling toxins, waste, and other unwanted materials. Because the lymphatic assists with the expelling of toxins, if it is not functioning properly, your skin may suffer from acne, loss of elasticity, and premature aging. It may also develop an overall flaky texture.

Unlike your cardiovascular system, the lymphatic system does not have a pump (i.e., the heart); it relies on you to get it going, but stimulating it is easier than you may think. Exercise is the number one way to do this, as regular muscle contraction stimulates the movement of our lymphatic fluid. Lymphatic massage is also a good option, as it utilizes techniques that contribute to healthy lymphatic drainage. However, the easiest way is to dry brush.

Dry brushing is an ancient practice of self-care that you should incorporate into your daily skin-care routine, done ideally before your daily shower (that way, you wash off all the dead skin cells you have loosened). And although you may have heard of dry brushing, you may not know how to start.

To begin, you need a good dry brush, one that is high quality and has natural bristles. The bristles should feel stiff to the touch but not hard. Try to find a brush with a long handle so that you can reach your back and other hard-to-reach places.

You want to begin with your feet, including the soles of your feet, and move the brush in small circular motions, moving toward the heart. This way is best for circulation and for your lymphatic system. Make sure to include legs, arms, chest, back, and stomach. However, it is best to avoid sensitive areas, unless you have a brush for delicate skin. It should be firm pressure but not cause you any pain—you are not scrubbing. Your skin will be pinkish when done. If your skin is red, raw, and irritated, you were applying way too much pressure, so lighten up!

Spend anywhere from five to twenty minutes dry brushing. It feels great, so enjoy it! When your lymphatic system is functioning well, you should notice clearer skin. It is simply amazing how connected the body and all of its systems are.

After your dry-brushing session, your skin will be exfoliated. You will have clearer pores and may even notice a reduction in cellulite!

Drinking a tea that is detoxifying, like red clover, lemon balm, dandelion, or another detox tea, upon arising in the morning will provide a helpful boost to the daily function of your lymphatic system.

Breath Work

Breath work is a practice of breathing consciously and with intent. It's known to increase well-being, reduce stress, balance systems, help with PTSD, and help with cleansing old emotions, pain, and trauma.

Breath is what keeps us alive, yet we rarely focus on or even think about breathing. When you become conscious of your breath, you can do deep-breathing patterns that are beneficial to the body. Most people breathe a shallow breath without even realizing it, and their bodies lack the life force they could be receiving if they practiced a deeper breath pattern.

In Hawaiian culture, the life force of a person is called *mana*. In yogi practices, they refer to it as *prana*. This life force can be strengthened with breath work. As we deeply breathe in different patterns, we clean out old, trapped emotions, stress, and trauma. It allows the body to regenerate. When you give your body the much-needed oxygen it is lacking, it can do wonders! Your skin will glow from the life force (mana) and breath being restored.

Not only is breath work amazing for your skin, health, and well-being, but it *feels* amazing as you engage in deep, controlled breath. People report spiritual visions, tingling sensations, euphoria, crying out old pain, overwhelming joy or laughter, and so many other positive experiences. I like to imagine the breath moving through all my organs, loosening up old, trapped emotions, and oxygenating my cells.

My first breath-work session was with a rebirther. It was very emotional, and I cried very hard. I saw family members who had hurt me, and I was able to forgive them during the session. It was unbelievable and unexpected. I had read a book about rebirthing, and I decided to try a session. I was skeptical until I experienced the undeniable power of breathing the right way.

This practice can be beneficial even from one session, but doing breath work daily can be a lifelong practice of wellness. Some people even tape their mouths shut at night when they sleep to ensure they are breathing deeply through the nose and not with an open mouth. An open mouth while sleeping can close off the throat and prevent a deep breath pattern in your sleep. When you breathe properly all night in your sleep state, you will wake up with more energy, a clearer mind, and an overall feeling of well-being.

There are breath-work classes, coaches, online videos, and books. Set your alarm each day to take a few minutes for breath work—it's a true life-changer, and I strongly recommend breath work. Not only will you feel more relaxed and focused, but your skin will glow from all the life-giving oxygen you've been missing out on.

Gua Sha

Gua sha is a traditional treatment in some Eastern cultures for rejuvenating skin and tissue and for facial lifting. It is a growing trend in the United States. The concept is that by scraping the skin in certain patterns and motions with a specially shaped tool—usually made from jade or some other precious stone—you can improve the health of your skin. Gua sha is known to help oxygenate blood and stimulate new blood flow. Any time we have an increase in blood flow, it promotes healing. The stimulation promotes cell turnover and skin regeneration. Gua sha can be beneficial for aging, pigmentation, breakouts, scarring, inflammation, and overall skin health. If used correctly, it can also promote lymphatic drainage and health. This treatment can be done anywhere on the body. It is amazing for the back of the legs, helping with cellulite and lymph flow.

You can have this treatment done professionally by a skin-care professional, or you can do it yourself at home. You can do this every day if you want. I didn't use this treatment in my spa, but now I wish that I had used this simple yet very effective skin-rejuvenating treatment. I just recently learned about this technique, and I am so hooked!

I like to wash my face in the evening and lie in bed with my gua sha tool—using a very hydrating organic oil—and treat myself to a wonderful, anti-aging facial treatment. The nights I do this, I wake up with hydrated, glowing skin. It's truly a noticeable result.

Please find a gua sha tool that does not support animal cruelty! Some manufacturers offer tools made of buffalo horn, so make sure you opt for a tool that uses a natural stone, such as quartz, jade, or Odacité crystal. There are different shapes and levels of sharpness. Start off with a classic shape and sharpness, and you can graduate into more professional levels of this treatment when you feel comfortable.

If you get a gua sha treatment done professionally, at an advanced level it can leave bruising and redness due to the blood stimulation. This is considered a wound response, as the increase in blood flow promotes healing. People even use this treatment for muscle pain on the back. Again, the increase of blood flow promotes healing in all ways.

Below are the instructions and a pattern for you to follow if you decide to incorporate this treatment into your at-home skin-care regime:

Step 1. Cleanse the desired area of treatment with an organic cleanser.
Step 2. Exfoliate lightly to ensure product delivery.
Step 3. Use a toner to restore natural pH.
Step 4. Use your gua sha tool to scrape the skin in the patterns that are most beneficial to the specific area you are treating.

Below is the pattern for a gua sha facial treatment.

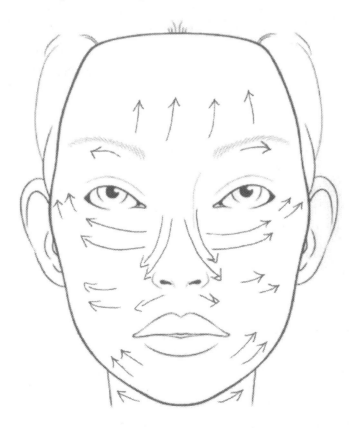

Facial Cupping

Facial cupping is a facial treatment that uses small, soft cups to gently pull blood into the areas underneath the cup. It saturates the tissue with fresh blood, promoting healing and new blood vessel formation. This practice is deeply ingrained in Chinese medicine, but some of the oldest pictorial records are dated back to Egyptian times.

The vacuum-like suction results in micro-trauma and tearing, separating the different layers of tissue. Just like some other treatments I mention, it is a wound-response technique that floods the area with white blood cells and platelets, promoting new tissue growth.

Unlike traditional body cupping that leaves behind cupping marks, facial cupping does not leave marks, if done correctly. People report improved complexions and a brighter skin tone. Reduction of fine lines and hyperpigmentation is also a benefit from facial cupping. Someone with acne can benefit from this treatment, as it also helps regulate oil production. I have seen some great results from facial cupping, especially the glow you get from doing it regularly. Use it on a saggy jawline or loose skin on your neck for noticeable results as well.

The great thing about this noninvasive facial treatment is that you can do it at home. The facial cups are inexpensive. It also feels so wonderful. We hold so much tension in our faces, and this is a great way to relieve stress in the face. Do it on your forehead lines instead of Botox for a surprisingly noticeable result.

Facial cupping at home

What you will need:

- Small, medium, and large facial cups (different sizes for different areas of the face)
- Cleanser
- Scrub
- Organic nourishing oil

Follow the following steps:

1. Wash your face with your favorite organic cleanser.
2. Do a light exfoliation to remove any dead skin cells.
3. Pat skin dry, and apply a natural organic toner to restore pH.
4. Massage your face with your hands to relieve preliminary tension.
5. Apply your nourishing oil to area.
6. Find the cup that fits that area of the face. For instance, the forehead and cheeks would use a larger cup. Around the eyes, nose, and chin would use a smaller cup.
7. Start on the chin and around the mouth and move in an upward, circular motion. Only leave the cup in place for a few seconds. Move over the entire face.

You can have a facial cupping treatment every day if you want or just a few times a week. Do it lightly if you want to do it daily. I suggest doing it at night before bed—in case any minor redness occurs. You can sleep it off and wake up looking rested and refreshed! Drink a big glass of lemon or coconut water to help with hydration, and the next morning you will be glowing.

Combining gua sha and facial cupping is very stimulating, and combining them can be done once a week as a more advanced home treatment. Just remember to never to do *any* treatment over broken or wounded skin. You can do it over acne, as long as there are no open wounds.

Grounding/Earthing

The average person wakes up on a bed and then steps onto a carpet, hardwood, or tile floor. When they are ready to go outside, they put on shoes with a rubber, plastic, or other synthetic sole between their feet and the earth. They go about their business and return home to take off their shoes and place them again on the carpet, hardwood, or tile floor. Day after day, they miss out on the earth's charge. The earth is alive and full of an energy that we are part of. When we never connect to the earth through grounding, or earthing, we can get very sick.

Think of it as if you are a battery and the earth is a charger. All animals and humans need to be grounded. There are so many environmental toxins, like radiation and electromagnetic fields. When we ground ourselves, we help the body to clean out these stressors.

Earthing is where you stand barefoot on the earth and allow the connection to happen. The negatively charged free electrons that flood the land, oceans, rivers, waterfalls, and even lightning are beneficial to us; we need them to be healthy.

Humans used to walk barefoot on the earth and sleep on the ground. The further we get from nature, the more our bodies suffer. The earth is like a big battery, getting recharged with negative electrons thousands of times per minute. That's why you feel so good at the beach, in the mountains, or next to a lake or waterfall—you are being charged up!

I have an indoor kitty, who is my love. She cannot go outside where I live—there are lots of coyotes and other wildlife that might see her as a snack—but I let her out every morning into my courtyard, where there is one small patch of earth under a palm tree. All the other ground is covered in pavement and concrete. She will always lie down on that patch of earth and stay there the entire time she is outside. She is earthing, or grounding, and charging up her cute little kitty body. It's so cool to watch how happy she gets and how much energy she has after going outside. It makes me think of all the kitties who never get to connect with the earth.

It's the same for us; we need to be connected to the earth. Make it a point to walk barefoot on the earth as much as you possibly can. Sit on the grass, stand on the sand, lie on the dirt! Charge yourself.

You can find lots of amazing grounding tools if you have a busy life. Grounding sheets are great because they ground you all night while you are sleeping, and that is when the body is healing and regenerating. Some people use a grounding rod or other grounding devices. Of course, standing or lying directly on the earth is best, but do what you can do. You will start to feel more energy; many people report better sleep. Lose the shoes, and get out there and connect to the earth as much as you can!

Epsom and Mineral Salt Baths

A good Epsom salt bath can do wonders. Many believe that Epsom salt is a great tool for helping the body to relax and draw out toxins. The name *Epsom* comes from a saline spring located in Surrey, England, where the compound first was discovered after being distilled from water.

Epsom salt is not like table salt. It is a mineral compound derived from magnesium and sulfate. The sulfate is great for drawing out toxins and flushing the liver. The magnesium is what helps the muscles relax. Taking an Epsom salt bath is an amazing way to get a daily dose of magnesium as well—it's my favorite way.

Magnesium is important to our health, but unfortunately, most people are highly deficient in magnesium. Magnesium is an essential mineral that helps to keep our bones strong and regulate our blood pressure. In the nervous system, magnesium is important for optimal nerve transmission and neuromuscular coordination. It also helps to protect against *excitotoxicity* from food additives and chemicals.

In short, magnesium can be a great tool for helping your skin to detox and also to help your mood stay calm and stabilized. That means less stress and beautiful skin from an amazing night of sleep.

It is important to make sure you use high-quality natural Epsom salt with no added chemicals, fragrances, or any other additives. Good, clean Epsom salt can really make your bath time a wonderful, calming experience. I like to take mine before bed, so my muscles and my mind are relaxed.

What about the Skin on the Rest of My Body?

Part of looking healthy and young is keeping the skin on your face smooth and supple. But what about the skin on the rest of our bodies—on our arms, legs, stomach, chest, and back?

Remember that your skin is an organ, and it is important to take care of all the skin on your entire body—even your buns! You should treat all your skin equally.

Early in my career as an aesthetician, I wondered why there was hand-and-body lotion as well as face lotion. I believe the reason that the skin on your face and neck age faster is that it is exposed to the environment more than any other part of the body. You also move the facial skin and muscles thousands of times a day from facial expressions, talking, squinting, and frowning. Many women, in particular, smother their precious skin with beauty creams and serums that are filled with harmful ingredients that are absorbed right into the bloodstream. Then the liver has to filter out those invaders.

Your face will age first, but do not be fooled by the slower aging of the rest of your skin. It will catch up with you if you don't take care of it. Exfoliating the skin on the rest of your body is important. Using a natural organic oil or cream that has no chemicals is very important for your internal health as well. Your body is a much larger area than only your face, and that means more product to absorb into the body. Make sure the body products you choose are super-clean. That includes your body washes, scrubs, body creams, and oils.

Earlier in this book, I discussed how the liver plays a major role in skin health and how skin-care products that are not food-based actually age the skin in the long run—all the skin, all over the body. By smothering your face with chemical-based products, you actually age the skin all over your body, including your face.

I mention in the liver section that sometimes these chemical-based products can seem to give you an instant result, so you will believe and swear they are working. In reality, these products have plumping agents in them or fillers that can artificially plump the skin. Or they have exfoliating properties that can take off a few dead layers that have been sitting there for a while and make the skin immediately brighten. The damage from these types of products comes over time. With daily use, they will clog up the liver, disrupt hormones, and so on. When the liver isn't functioning at full potential, you will age faster—the more our livers are burdened, the faster we age.

Treat the skin on the rest of your body the same as you would treat your face or neck. I suggest using natural organic oils on your body. Grapeseed oil is amazing for skin, as well as almond oil, jojoba, coconut, castor—the list goes on and on of wonderful oils that can nourish your skin. If you're not a fan of oil, you could use organic body creams, as long as they are clean and free of anything other than nature.

CHAPTER 13

Skin Issues

What Is a Wrinkle?

Did you know a wrinkle is a scar?

A wrinkle is a fold or crease in the skin where collagen has broken down, and it has lost its elasticity. This means it does not bounce back after years of making the same movements. The tissue has broken down and created a fold or crease—a scar.

Can wrinkles be reversed?

Yes! I have seen deep wrinkles corrected from diet and the right facial treatments.

Diet is, in my opinion, 80 percent of skin care. Remember that our skin is alive; it's a living organ, and it needs nutrients to stay healthy.

I have had clients who looked way younger in their forties than they did in their twenties, just because they started eating life-giving foods, rather than life-taking foods. They have a brighter glow and look more youthful at an older age.

Is it possible to reverse some of the damage from a poor past lifestyle?

Yes, for sure! I have seen it many times. It all goes back to the liver.

When our liver functions at top performance, then our other organs don't take on the load of toxicity. We have enough toxic chemicals constantly bombarding us daily; the last thing we should do is eat more of them and slather them on our skin. So yes, wrinkles most certainly can be reversed.

Prevent them in the first place by staying hydrated and full of living waters from fruit—that's a strong defense against dry, wrinkled skin. Cutting out dehydrating foods and toxic products will give your skin a chance to restore its luster. Exfoliating is also a great tool in fighting wrinkles because you are speeding up your cell turn-over. Any way you look at it, wrinkles can be avoided with a clean lifestyle and lots of hydration.

Acne

Suffering from acne can be devastating. Nobody understands how someone with acne feels. I know because I have held people in my arms, crying from the emotional pain they feel from looking in the mirror at the inflamed face that is looking back. It angers me to no end that few skin care professionals will address someone's diet when suggesting treatment for acne. Acne is caused by viruses and bacteria trapped under the skin and lymph nodes that thrive off bad food, bad products, stress, and hormones. Often, someone with a toxic liver also may experience breakouts. In my career, I have helped so many people with acne. I'm going to talk about all my little secrets to fight acne in this section. Some of them may sound silly or useless, but they come from many years of trial and error with my clients.

One of the first things I do with acne clients is recommend they change their diets. They should cut out processed sugar, gluten, dairy, MSG (including MSG under other hidden names), corn, citric acid, anything GMO, and bad oils, especially vegetable and canola oils. I then suggest that they start high doses of a good, clean vitamin C (as I discussed earlier in the book).

Adding antiviral supplements is helpful when combating acne. Things like lemon balm, garlic, and oregano oil are some of my top suggestions. Water plays a very important role in keeping the cells hydrated and helping to flush the toxins out of the system. I suggest adding freshly squeezed lemon to your water. It adds life to your water, and lemon is also amazing at flushing the system naturally. Adding lots of fruit to your diet is also a powerful way to fight acne. Fruit is life-giving and can help the body kill off unwanted pathogens. It also is a wonderful way to hydrate the body, and God knows we all could use a little more hydration. Most people are chronically dehydrated and have no idea. Fruit is beneficial to your skin—lots of fruit equals beautiful skin! I've seen it with my own eyes.

Cutting out the bad food and adding antiviral supplements, fruit, and lots of clean water is a huge start to cleaning up acne. You will notice changes in the first week. Sometimes, there may be a purge after you start. Remember that it's temporary, and you will get through it. The purge is good. It means it's all coming out and clearing out. Just keep pushing through it. You can add topical skin gels like colloidal silver; tamanu oil is also great for acne and scarring.

If you have been told that you have acne because of a hormonal imbalance, it may be somewhat true. I believe if you balance the body as a whole, the hormones will also start to balance out. Doing these key things will help your hormones balance out naturally. Once the body has a chance to clean out and isn't working so hard on fighting all the bad stuff we put in it, the body can regulate. This is a very simple explanation to what really happens, but it's all you need to know to start making changes. Doing the 777 Skin Detox plan that is mentioned later in this book is recommended for someone struggling with acne.

Rosacea

When doctors can't figure out why your skin is red, inflamed, and ruddy, they just call it rosacea. Over the years, so many clients have come to me after going from doctor to dermatologist to aesthetician, just to be told they have rosacea. Most likely, that red complexion accompanied with pimples, pustules, or broken capillaries is due to inflammation in the body.

Inflammation in the body is directly linked to whatever you are putting in or on your body: food, alcohol, sugar, medications, stress, and so forth. Logically, it makes sense that your diet would have a huge impact on rosacea, right? That's not what the medical skin-care professionals are telling you, though. They want to prescribe a chemical-based gel that will clear up the redness.

What?

If our skin, our largest detox organ, is suffering with a red rash, wouldn't that tell us there is an underlying issue in our bodies? If we know that rosacea is caused from inflammation, then why would we put another chemical irritant on our largest organ? There may be an immediate calming down of the skin from these metro-gels but the long-term effect of them will rear its head, and the next time your rosacea comes back, it will come back worse.

I've seen it so many times. The rosacea won't go away until we get to the root of the skin issue in the body and reduce internal inflammation. It's possible to cure rosacea for good! I've helped many clients get rid of this frustrating skin condition. If you are suffering from skin redness and have been told that you have rosacea, focus on an anti-inflammatory diet and lifestyle. Here's what that looks like:

- No alcohol—this is a big one for red, ruddy complexions
- No sugar
- No gluten
- Low fat
- Lots of fruit
- Lots of greens
- Low stress
- High doses of vitamin C
- Spirulina
- Turmeric
- Curcumin
- Plant-based omegas: chia, flax, avocado—not too much; too much of even good fat is hard on your liver
- No dairy—this is a must!

If you adhere to the above, week after week, your skin will calm down and start to glow. I have offered these suggestions to my clients with rosacea for many years with much success. It takes a little discipline and a little time, but you will be amazed by the results. Following the 777 Total Skin Detox plan is recommended for rosacea.

Liver Spots

Liver spots are those brown spots that pop up most commonly on your hands, face, and arms. They are a tiny bit raised and often have a slight texture to them, although sometimes they are completely flat.

What are these spots, and why is it so hard to get rid of them? From my years of experience, these stubborn spots are directly linked to the liver and the kidneys. They are a sure sign that your organs are not filtering out the bad stuff at the optimal level. I have seen people change their diets, and these spots vanish!

I believe these little warning spots are a symptom of a toxic overload in the detox organs. Things like pathogens, viruses, heavy metals, plastics, and other harmful pollutants are getting into the blood and creating toxic blood, which causes oxidation in the skin pigmentation. It affects the thyroid and the adrenal glands, which are the precursor for the hormones that create melanocytes, which, in turn, create pigmentation. This is the main cause of melasma and other pigment-related issues.

Our adrenaline plays a huge role in melasma. Basically, when we have a burden on the liver and kidneys, they can't do their normal functions. Things get out of balance, and it becomes a chain reaction. No one knows the exact events that take place in the system to create these skin pigmentation issues. I do know that when the diet is cleaned up and replaced with living foods that are alive and are full of the nutrients and antiviral properties that we were meant to eat, the spots can and do vanish.

Broken Capillaries, Spider Veins, and What to Do

Broken capillaries on the face can give you a ruddy complexion and definitely age you. You may be more prone to these the older you get because the capillary walls get thinner and weaker. Age isn't always a factor, though. I have seen many young people with lots of broken vessels, usually people who are heavy drinkers, smokers, or drug users or who have a poor diet.

The good news is that the broken vessels can be repaired and prevented by having a healthy blood flow as a result of cleaning up your diet and getting enough of certain vitamins, such as vitamin K and vitamin C.

When the blood is thick from a buildup of toxins, other pathogens, and chronic dehydration, it can actually stretch out the veins and capillaries, resulting in broken vessels, as well as enlarged vessels. That's when you see varicose veins, spider veins, and broken blood vessels. I believe they are signs of stagnant blood flow.

When the liver has a heavy burden from all the toxins we ingest daily, on top of a high-fat diet, the bloodstream becomes thick and goopy. The heart then has to pump this toxic blood, bogging down the entire vascular system. It just makes sense, if you really think about what is going on.

The solution to the red spider veins that are messing up that flawless complexion you're after is to clean up the bloodstream. We do that by cleaning out our livers.

Yes, it all goes back to the liver. Our liver is our hero, fighting to clean up all the things that do not belong in our system. Our livers get overloaded, and our blood becomes toxic. If you suffer from broken capillaries, varicose veins, and spider veins, here are some tips to start reducing the present ones and preventing any future ones:

Hydrate, hydrate, hydrate! Drinking clean water with lemon is one of the best ways to hydrate and also help to clean out the liver.

Eating lots of fruits and vegetables that are hydrating and full of nutrients also will help to clean out the toxins in the liver as well as the bloodstream.

I love neem oil, garlic, turmeric, aloe vera, and burdock root; they are great ways to help clean up the bloodstream.

Taking a vitamin K supplement and a vitamin C supplement is a great way to support the vascular system.

These tricks not only can help the capillaries on your face, but you will notice that spider veins on your legs and other body parts will start to disappear. You will also prevent the appearance of future ones. I use the thin spider veins on my leg to gauge my health when they start to get worse. I know I need to eat better, and then, within a few weeks, they will lighten up and start to disappear. It really is cool that I have this kind of control over my health, just by my food choices.

Warts and Growths

Warts and growths are becoming more common, and my clients who seek a solution to them seem to be getting younger and younger. You can burn a wart off, but it most likely will come back if the underlying condition is not addressed.

I wanted to find out the causes of warts and skin growths so that I could better recommend to my clients how to get rid of them or, better yet, how to prevent them.

I started digging and researching, and one of the things that kept jumping out to me was a zinc deficiency. So many of us are deficient in minerals and vitamins due to our poor diets and depleted soil. Zinc deficiency, along with magnesium deficiency, seems to be very common. I realized that when I suggested zinc to clients, not only did their acne improve, but their skin growths and warts started to disappear.

We know that warts are viral, so it makes sense that antiviral supplements would be a cure for them. Well, it turns out that taking a zinc supplement not only helps diminish skin growths and warts, but it also helps kill pathogens in the body.

Zinc is a virus-killer. The antiviral and antibacterial properties make zinc a powerful defense against acne, but it's a powerful supplement to add to your life, even if you do not have warts or skin growths. When pathogens take over our body systems, it can be a snowball effect of health and skin problems. Zinc is a strong weapon against viral invaders that cause our systems to break down.

I suggest adding an organic zinc sulfate to your daily regimen; hopefully, you will not only watch skin growths disappear, but you will feel more energy and more focused and alive, and you will improve your overall well-being and health. Some foods that are high in zinc are microgreens, parsley, onions, raw honey, and artichokes. But keep in mind that even these foods that typically are high in zinc often are depleted from the lack of nutrients in the soil.

Children's Skin Rashes

Sometimes babies are born with skin problems. It's heartbreaking to see beautiful babies with psoriasis or eczema covering their new baby skin. If your child suffers with a skin problem, there is hope to clear it up and keep it cleared up for good. I do not believe that it's incurable. Although many will disagree with this opinion, I still want to share my experience on the topic.

I have four daughters who are currently twenty-two, twenty, twelve and three years old. I can say that I've seen it all, as far as kids' stuff goes.

As a child, my oldest daughter, Georgia Rae, suffered for years with rashes on her hands; they were dry to the point that they would bleed. We learned in her teens, after she was diagnosed with SIBO and Crohn's disease, that these rashes were from her toxic liver and poor digestion. Although I tried my hardest to always feed my kids healthy and organic food, I missed a major factor when it came to my kids' skin health: the liver and fat.

We had previously started a Keto-type diet with high fat. Although we were eating organic and only healthy fats, the fat intake was just too heavy of a load on her liver. They don't teach this in school or report on it in the mainstream media when it comes to skin health. I learned what I know only by trial and error with family, clients, my kiddos, and myself.

Georgia was finally diagnosed with Crohn's after we searched all over Los Angeles for answers. We went to conventional doctors, homeopaths, nutritionists, UCLA specialists, and anyone who claimed they knew the answers. After two long years of Georgia's suffering and being very sick, we finally got the answers that we had hoped for.

We stopped most of the fat intake and went completely vegan, only eating fats found in nature from avocados, nuts, and seeds. Even then, we still were careful of how much fat she would intake. It was like a miracle! Her rashes cleared up, and her symptoms slowly started to disappear. I had been taught—and I believed for most of my career—that fat reduced inflammation, that your brain ran on fat, and so forth. Hence, the whole paleo, ketogenic diet, which, by the way, is a catastrophe for your health and your skin in the long term. Too much fat equals poor health, as we have now learned.

You should never trick your body into thinking it's starving. It will stress your system and actually age you.

Anyway, it all started to click for our family and for me as a skin-care professional. If our livers are toxic, they cannot filter out the daily stressors of life, and when we eat so much fat, our livers get clogged up and stagnant. It's like a backed-up sewer system. Our skin, being our largest organ, suffers from the toxic overload in the body. You can be thin and look fit, but inside can be another story.

I showed my girls a cool experiment using two sponges. I dripped oil in one and fruit juice in the other. The oil dried in the sponge, making it hard and brittle. The fruit juice, however, kept the sponge soft and porous.

Although, ultimately, you cannot compare a sponge to your amazing liver, it's just a simple example of how lots of fat and oils can clog up the liver. As discussed earlier in this book, there is a direct liver/skin connection, and very few in the skin-care industry know it. It seems simple to understand, yet I'm often surprised that people just don't get it.

Let's just imagine a filter. If we add fat, butter, and oil to the filter, what happens? It's clogged up, and it can't function right. Now, let's add fresh water, enzymatic fruits, and vegetables that actually *dissolve* gunk. What happens now? I hope it is clicking.

If your kids suffer from skin issues, switch their diet with lots of fresh fruit—citrus fruits are great, as are mangoes and bananas—and watch things change fast. I like to throw a huge handful of spinach in the kids' smoothies, and they never even taste it.

If you are a breastfeeding mother and have a baby with skin rashes, try changing your diet by cutting out all the bad stuff we talked about, and watch your baby's skin clear up. When it comes time to give your baby a bottle after breastfeeding, please consider not giving a conventional milk-based formula. Try a homemade version of a formula, and watch your baby thrive and glow.

I breastfed my youngest for two years and then switched to a banana, date, and spinach blend for her milk substitute. She loved it, and her bowel movements happened four to five times a day. The perfect blend of glucose, vitamins, and minerals were a better option than a milk-based formula for my little one. Depending on how bad the issues are, you should see some changes after a week of a fruit and veggie diet for your little munchkin. Of course you should always check with your pediatrician for any decisions you make for your family.

CHAPTER 14

Supplements for Skin Health

Using dietary supplements for healthy skin is important because we lack so many vital nutrients in our foods. Each issue people face with their skin is different. I have made a list of supplements that I have found to be beneficial for people suffering with problematic skin. These supplements can also be taken as a preventive measure and to maintain beautiful skin.

I offer amounts, but be sure to check with the recommended dosages and always check with your health care professional before taking any supplements.

For acne and skin rashes
Vitamin C ester (3000–5000 mg/day)
Zinc—liquid zinc sulfate only (one dropper/day)
Cat's claw (one full dropper or dosage/day)
Celery juice (16–32 oz./day)
Oregano oil (1 capsule/day)
Hawaiian spirulina (one serving/day—add to a smoothie)

For rosacea, skin rashes, and aging
Vitamin C ester (3000–5000 mg/day)
Zinc—liquid zinc sulfate (one dropper/day)

> L-lysine (500–1000 mg/day)
> Celery juice (16–32 oz./day)
> DHA—*vegan only*; no fish oil (2 capsules/day)

Raw Honey

Raw honey—unfiltered, organic, and clean, like nature intended—can be such a healing and medicinal food, as well as a beauty product. Topically, it can help aid in healing scars, acne, dry skin, infections, and so much more. Honey is antiviral, antibacterial, hydrating, and full of nutrients, and it's truly a superfood, internally. Use it in your masks and your hair, and while you are at it, take a big spoonful internally!

I grow my own honey, and it's wonderful. There are new ways of harvesting your own honey, depending on where you live. Here in the state of California, they have decided that kept bees are way less aggressive than wild bees. It's a great way to help keep bees on the planet. Bees are in danger, and we need to protect these little guys because without them, we can't survive either.

Vitamin C—Internally

Vitamin C is so important for skin and tissue repair. Vitamin C is not only an antioxidant but an anti-inflammatory as well. Vitamin C helps to repair tissue and promotes new collagen and elastin. It also is excellent for boosting your immune system and fighting off free radicals. It is legion when it comes to skin health.

I often recommended high doses of vitamin C in my practice for clients suffering from acne, rosacea, or aging skin. The vitamin C you choose is also important—I cannot stress this enough. Most of the vitamin C manufactured today comes from genetically modified corn. It is synthetic and serves no benefit to the body. Actually, many experts will tell you that GMO vitamin C is harmful to you. Try to avoid ascorbic acid. Ascorbic acid is the synthetic vitamin C, typically derived from GMO corn.

Pick a whole-food–based C that is non-GMO. I have listed my favorite vitamin C supplements on my website. You can also make sure to eat lots of fruits that are high in vitamin C, like papayas, strawberries, kiwi, pineapple, and mango, just to name a few.

You could be depleted of vitamin C if you haven't eaten a lot of fruits and veggies or aren't taking a supplement. I like to take around 5000 mg a day of vitamin C ester. I suggest starting with a lower dose of 2000 mg a day of organic, non-GMO vitamin C ester and add 250–500 mg until you start to get a little bit of loose bowels. If you get loose bowels, you will know to back off a little and take a little less. If you don't get loose bowels, it means you really need it.

This is my opinion, and it is what I have suggested to many clients over the years with great success. Vitamin C is such a powerful nutrient when it comes to skin health. If you are deficient, you will not believe the glow you get once you start taking it. I call it the vitamin C glow! Your gums, hair, and nails will thank you too.

Zinc

Zinc may be one of the most important supplements for skin health. Your body uses up zinc quickly, especially if you are fighting a virus. Most people have viruses, even if they are not feeling ill. Viruses hide in our organs and are triggered by poor diet and pathogens that the viruses feed on and then grow stronger. When we take antivirals, we lower the viral load. Zinc is also important for liver function; even though the liver stores zinc, we can become deficient due to our lifestyles and lack of nutrients in our food and soil. I have watched people who suffer with acne start a zinc supplement, and the acne vanished. Sometimes it's that simple; sometimes not. Zinc is a powerful friend to the liver and to the immune system and is critical for skin health and overall well-being. Make sure to take a zinc sulfate. It has proven to work the best for skin health for my clients. A liquid zinc sulfate is best for optimal skin health. Check with your health care provider for recommended dosage. A good tip is to make sure you take zinc after a meal because it can cause an upset tummy if taken without food.

Spirulina

Spirulina is a powerful superfood. It is a great source of protein and iron and is full of vitamins and minerals. Spirulina is often considered one of the most nutrient-dense foods on the planet. Adding spirulina to your diet can improve your skin health tremendously. The high chlorophyll content helps to cleanse the blood, and it's also great for helping to eliminate heavy metals, which are a major cause of skin pigmentation. Heavy metals oxidize over time and cause all kinds of skin issues.

Make sure to get a clean product. Hawaiian spirulina is the best for a dried product. You also can get fresh-grown spirulina. My local farmers' market has a fresh, organically grown spirulina, and it's wonderful! You can order it online to be shipped on ice as well. Add it to your smoothies, and you will never even taste it. The fresh spirulina is actually almost tasteless. I add it to my family's smoothies so they get lots of iron, protein, and other life-giving nutrients, including chlorophyl.

Antivirals

We live in a virus-infested world. Wherever they came from is not the concern anymore. The real concern is that they are here, mutating and affecting us all. No one is immune to picking up a virus. Viruses attack our immune systems, our nerves, and our organs, and that's when we start to have skin-health issues. We have been told that our immune systems attack our bodies. New information indicates that the body will never attack itself; it's the viruses that attack us and make our bodies sick. (You won't hear this in the mainstream medical industry.)

Everything we put in our mouths or on our bodies will either feed the viral load or kill off the viral load. I like to think of it as a bank. When we eat corn, soy, bad oils, gluten, eggs, and processed foods, we feed the viruses living in our bodies, especially eggs. Viruses love eggs. They are their favorite food. When we eat fruit (fruit is antiviral), leafy greens, herbs, and vegetables, we aid in killing off the viral load. Supplementing with antivirals is a great way to help keep the evil viruses we face daily under control. I made a list of antivirals that are important for keeping skin issues under control. We already talked about zinc in its own section. I believe zinc is the most important antiviral supplement you can take for your skin and for protection against viral bugs.

CHAPTER 15

Makeup

The moment you wake up—stop before you put on that makeup!

What a vicious cycle makeup can be. We wear it to look better but it could be aging us on every level and making us look worse in the long run, if we use toxic makeup.

Your makeup could be harming you in so many ways. One is topically, by smothering your skin with plastic-like chemicals that prevent your living organ from breathing and functioning in its normal state.

Another is that many of the chemicals found in today's conventional makeup brands are able to absorb through the skin. With long-term exposure, they can wreak havoc on the endocrine system, create hormonal imbalance, and even make you sick. Things like pesticides and heavy metals have been found in some of these makeups.

There is also the danger of the counterfeit makeups that no one really knows about. These makeups are so toxic that people have been hospitalized after having certain reactions to some of the chemicals in them. People want things cheap, and they don't think about the long-term effects on the body and skin or on the environment by producing such toxic chemicals.

The very makeup you are using to cover up your hormonal melasma may very well be contributing to it!

Makeup ages you, literally, and it also ages your appearance. When we were twelve and wore a lot of makeup, it made us look older. Nothing changes when we are twenty, thirty, forty, and onward; we also look older with makeup.

Try to use as little foundation as possible. Just accent the eyes, cheeks, and lips with a bit of color, if you feel uncomfortable being completely bare. You'll look younger and fresher, and your skin will be so happy that it can breathe.

Luckily, we have options. The first suggestion is to get your skin as healthy as possible, so you will need little to no makeup in the first place.

If you love to express yourself through the art of makeup, you will be happy to know there is an uprising of indie makeup brands emerging on the market. Brands are creating nontoxic, clean makeup that is vegan and environmentally friendly. Not only will you do your skin and body a favor, but you will be a part of the cure, fighting against the evil of these companies that have no regard for human life, animal life, or the life of our planet.

Buying organic, vegan, nontoxic makeup is just one way you can start to heal your skin and the planet. I have listed my favorite nontoxic makeup brands on my website. They work amazingly, and you can feel safe wearing them, especially if you are fighting an illness or are pregnant or nursing.

Brow Color

I include brow color in my list of small secrets that make a big difference because it can be a face-changer.

Thin, pale brows age you, with some exceptions.

Why? Because when we are young, our brows are unruly, natural, and thick. It's not until we get older and start tweezing and shaping that we lose the volume and natural wildness of our youthful brows. Keep your brows as thick as possible and as dark as possible for a youthful look. Even if you are blonde, I would go with a medium- to light-brown brow. If you are blonde with a blonde brow, you can lose your face without some definition. Unless you are going for that pale, high-fashion blonde-brow look—which I also love, but it seems harder to pull off—then stick to a darker brow. It's just a little trick for a youthful look.

If you have already tweezed your brows, and they have stopped growing, try a lash growth serum on your brows. Castor oil is amazing for hair-growth stimulation.

Also, once you start eating all the leafy greens, veggies, and fruits, you will be surprised by how fast all your hair grows. I have seen hair loss reversed by eating a plant-based diet. Sometimes, you may have a little hair loss before it starts to grow in full again. This is like your body's way of purging out all the old hair and making room for thicker, healthier hair. My hair grows like a weed when I eat a super-nutritious, plant-based diet. When I start slipping and eat poorly, I definitely see a huge difference in my hair quality.

CHAPTER 16

Exercise and Skin

Of course, exercise is good for us, but what kind of exercise is truly good for us? I see so many people exhausting their bodies and causing oxidative stress. Oxidative stress ages us! We have hard-core workout programs and high-protein diets that could age us more than we know. The problem is we see our muscles start to shape up, and we believe this means health. When you work out so hard that you can't sit down for three days, that is not anti-aging! That is causing stress to your body, and then your body uses the energy it needs in its overburdened system to clean itself out—to heal the torn muscles you have from your hard-core workout. More is not always better!

When you exercise, it should mimic the natural movements and motions that humans do. I have seen some of the most beautiful bodies from activities like swimming, biking, hiking, yoga, dance, ballet, martial arts, and other natural movements. Moving tractor tires over an obstacle course is not an average activity in which most humans, historically, have engaged.

Then, on top of the exhaustion, people burden their livers with high-protein diets. High-protein/high-fat diets clog up our livers, cause illness, and age our skin fast. Then add the oxidative stress from your hard-core workout, and things will not head in the right direction. Anthony William talks about this in his books, and I believe it with all my heart. When you see someone who looks really buffed out, often it's a layer of inflammation and swelling under the skin. It may look aesthetically pleasing to that individual, but internally, his or her health is suffering.

Eating lots of raw organic fruits and veggies will fuel muscles better than protein. Your liver is responsible for creating the protein that your body can use and recognize. We need the fruits and vegetables that contain the amino acids that are responsible for protein development in the body. The protein you consume in a powder or shake is not absorbed by the body and usually just means you've added more fat and burden to your poor liver.

The truth is that your brain runs on glucose, and your muscles need glucose to recover and develop. That's why people who eat lots of fruits and veggies have plumped-up skin and lean, toned muscles.

Think about it: if I feed myself living foods that are full of life versus dead fat and protein, what will the better outcome be? Unfortunately, people have been brainwashed by the media and supplement companies to believe that protein is needed to build muscle.

Did you know there are traces of protein in all kinds of fruit and veggies? It's the kind of protein your body craves. One way to prove this is to look at some of the top athletes in the world who are vegan. They look healthy, their skin is glowing, and their muscles are lean and toned. When our tissue is healthy from all the life-giving nutrients, we also look younger and more vibrant. Some of these athletes only eat raw foods on top of it. They *mono eat* (eat one type of fruit) for top performance. They report more energy and life force, and, in my professional opinion, they have the most beautiful skin. It really shows in their glow.

If you do hard-core workouts, listen to your body and look at what you are feeding your body to recover. I personally love ballet for a workout. It helps me stay flexible, lean, and balanced. There are lots of squats, bends, and arm movements. I get my heart rate up and sweat, but I do not feel like I'm going to throw up when I'm done.

Just listen to your body, do the research on what really fuels you, and don't age yourself from too much stress—physical or mental.

CHAPTER 17

Aesthetic Facial Treatments That Work

There are so many treatments for skin on the market now. I have listed the ones that I find safe from radiation and harmful chemicals. These are treatments you can feel safe doing, and there are no harmful side effects.

LED Light Therapy

I absolutely love LED light therapy. I used LED lights in my skin-care practice for years and I love it because I have seen such great healing results from it. When you couple oxygen and LED lights, the results are instantaneous.

The lights are set at a certain nanometer optimal for skin healing, which is red light at 660 nanometers. Your skin just glows! If you can find a place that offers LED red light therapy at 660 nanometers, I strongly suggest it for gorgeous skin. It speeds up your cell turnover and improves the general health of your skin. There are also some great new personal size LED devices that offer the same medical grade results.

LED light therapy is especially important before an event like a party or a wedding. I recommend it two days before an event for optimal results. LED therapy can also offer relief from inflammation and redness. You can benefit from LED therapy anywhere on the body. It's a wonderful thing to add into your skin health regimen.

Microneedling

Microneedling is a treatment that uses a roller or pen to make tiny tears in the skin. The tiny tears create a wound response and trigger healing and regeneration of the skin.

I love microneedling. If done right at home, you can incorporate it into your skin-care regime. You can purchase at-home microneedle rollers online. There are also microneedle pens available now for home use.

They come in different needle lengths. I suggest getting a set that has 0.5-, 1.0-, and 1.5-millimeter lengths. You can use the 1.5 on your cheeks, jowls, and the thicker-skinned areas of the face. You can use the 1.0 and .5 around the thinner areas, such as your neck and around your eyes.

The treatment can be repeated every twenty-one days. Our skin does a twenty-one-day cell turnover, and doing a light wound to the skin can help plump it up and stimulate new tissue. Waiting twenty-one days also gives the skin a chance to heal between treatments.

It is a bit uncomfortable the first few times you roll your face, but you will build up a tolerance.

There is a more professional version of microneedling with a pen that you can have done professionally. You can purchase an electric pen for home use as well. They are more expensive, but you can get a deeper treatment with a pen. Both the roller and the pen are safe, if used correctly. I have seen it deliver significant results for scarring, wrinkles, melasma, hyperpigmentation, and loose jowls and neck.

There are many tutorials and instructions online about how to microneedle with a roller or a pen at home. Please make sure you are clear on how to do this properly.

Supplies Needed for Microneedle Facial
Microneedle roller: .5, 1.0, and 1.5 mm or microneedle pen
Exfoliator
Cleanser
Anti-aging serum or vitamin C serum

Moisturizer or beauty oil

Dermaplaning

Dermaplaning is another amazing facial treatment that you can do yourself at home. It's not much different than shaving your face. If men can do it every day, women should be able to do it just as well! The only difference is that you will use a straight-edge blade, and you will remove not only unsightly hair but also layers of damaged skin cells, scarring, and superficial pigmentation. The best part is that you only have to do it once a month.

I love this treatment because it gives the skin such a sleek, smooth look and really helps if you wear makeup. You know what I mean if you have peach fuzz and you wear foundation—it's fuzz with makeup in it! I am all for keeping the fuzz and looking super-natural as well. I love that look too. At times, I have embraced my fuzz (I have a lot of it), and at other times, I have shaved my fuzz. It's whatever you prefer and feel good doing. Your hair will not grow back thicker unless you are dealing with hormonal hair growth patterns. If you're looking for a smooth, tight look, dermaplaning can be a great treatment.

Silicone Strips on Wrinkles

I have had three C-sections in my lifetime; each was harder than the last. One thing they all had in common was that they left me with a big scar on my lower abdomen.

I had my first two daughters in my twenties, my third daughter came to me in my thirties, and my fourth daughter in my early forties. I was lucky enough to have a wonderful doctor who was able to cut my old scars out and leave me with a beautifully done C-section scar after my last daughter. I had heard about silicone strips and how great they worked on scarring, and I thought I would give them a try. I tried it out, and I have to say that these things work!

My C-section scar is a very thin, white line now, and it looks great.

I know that it must have worked because I did not use these strips on the other C-section scars, and this last scar is clearly much less visible and smooth.

I had the epiphany of using them on facial wrinkles. Why not? They work on scars and wrinkles are scars. I started using the strips on my smile lines and chest lines. Now, I am a huge fan of silicone strips for deep wrinkles and lines, as well as superficial lines.

It takes discipline and memory to see the results, but if you do it nightly, you will see a difference in a few weeks. Of course, the smile lines come back with repeated smiling. I smile so often that it's just one of those things I have learned to accept. With beauty, it's an ongoing fight against aging.

Some companies now make silicone sheets specifically for facial parts. They work great, and if you have that one deep line that you really hate, you should give these a try.

CHAPTER 18

What Does Food Mean to You?

Why do we eat? We all know that we have to eat to stay alive. We were born into the world and had an instant instinct to eat, to consume a substance of nutrients to survive.

Another question to ask yourself is, why do you eat what you eat? Do you follow the same diet that your parents did? Do you follow trendy fad diets? What belief around food do you have, and where did that come from? You had no choice of what went into your body to survive when you were born. Maybe you were breastfed, or maybe you were given a formula. Maybe you were super lucky and were blessed to have a mother who believed food was the most important part of your life, and she herself ate a clean diet while you were in the womb. Maybe you were born before the 1970s and had a diet of whole foods, free from GMOs. If you were so lucky to have these advantages, then you may not have many skin issues, and you are ahead of the game on the quest for gorgeous skin. In my experience, however, I've seen that's not the case for most people. Most people and their parents never thought food was a big deal. It was something that they ate to survive and feel good or to celebrate with and never gave a thought of what it actually does to their health or bodies.

We innocently trusted the food companies that distributed the food. We saw entertaining ads that made us believe that we were buying something we needed, wanted, or would benefit from if we ate these foods. We never questioned that food could be the reason so many people are struggling with all types of skin problems, as well as health problems in general. It can be as simple as pigmentation. It could be dry skin or something more serious, like skin cancer. Things that seem like small, harmless skin issues are most likely a cry for help from your largest organ and is the alarm bell and a precursor of deeper issues to come.

Your skin is a great watchman of the body. It can give you signs that warn of other possible problems you may have internally. The skin can develop symptoms such as growths, pigmentation, acne, veins, rapid aging, wrinkles, sores, and rashes. These are all warning signs. A good example of this is warts. As I mention earlier in the book, I have seen a pattern around warts. It seems that they happen due to of a lack of minerals and nutrients, especially a zinc deficiency. If you have a wart, try taking zinc sulphate for a month, along with magnesium and proper hydration; most often, people watch their warts disappear. Because warts are viral, it also makes sense to take an antiviral supplement. Viral bugs cannot live in a body that has the proper balance of nutrients, minerals, enzymes, and all the other living information that communicates directly with the cells and organs. These viral bugs feed on bad food and toxins. When the bad stuff isn't there for the bugs (viruses, bacteria, fungi) to feed on, the bugs die off. The human body is similar to a computer that gets a virus and starts acting weird. Your computer may start off with a few faulty issues but will worsen over time, unless you clean up the bugs. It kind of works the same way with your body.

We can clearly see that people who eat living food are healthy, mentally and physically, but somehow, our food addictions and brainwashing from food companies overrides the evidence. We trust companies that have one intention—to make money. Before you look at the 7-7-7 skin detox in the next chapter and start the plan, remember that these foods are a blessing. You shouldn't feel deprived or that you are suffering. You are suffering when you consciously eat things that are disrupting the true essence of yourself and your health. Everything you do in your life is affected by your food. It is the foundation of your personality, your attitude, your sleep, your looks, your relationships, your energy, your eye and hair color, your skin tone, your nails, your sex drive, your perception of yourself, your memory, your happiness, and even your spirituality. It's important to realize the way in which food works with the human body and how more than just your skin is affected by your diet.

By adhering to the following diet, you will help to hydrate your skin and flood your body with vitamins, minerals, nutrients, and living food. You will lift your vibration and your energy. Feel the joy in this diet; I hope you choose to live this way for the rest of your life. It is true freedom of health and beautiful skin.

The 7-7-7 Detox Plan—Twenty-One Days to Healthy Skin

Week One: Days 1–7

Let go of sugar.
Let go of gluten.
Let go of soy.
Let go of dairy and eggs.
Let go of animal flesh.
Include at least one fruit/leafy green smoothie a day.
Include at least one green juice a day.
Include lemon water, 1 gallon a day

It sounds like a lot, but you can do this. It's not that hard to do if you have the right mindset. Remember that fruit is not white table sugar. You can eat as much fruit as you like on this skin detox. This is a game-changer when you are cleansing the body. If you have the glucose, vitamins, minerals, and nutrients from lots of fruit during this skin detox, you don't suffer, and you give your body what it needs to flush out the pathogens and to give your body the hydration it desperately needs. During these first days and beyond, you can enjoy big servings of fruit and not feel guilty! You can choose fruits as a meal or a snack. Eating an entire melon for breakfast is an example of a great breakfast on this detox. You won't gain weight unless you add a bunch of other foods that are not alive at the same time you are eating lots of fruit. Now, if you have pancakes for breakfast and then a bag of grapes on top of it, you most likely will gain weight. The idea here is not to add the fruit on top of your current diet; you are to replace your current diet with lots of fruit. Try to stick to one fruit at a time so your body can benefit from that particular fruit's information and nutritional benefits. For week one, you eliminate and get the body adjusted to giving up these no-no foods and replace the bad foods with living high-vibrational foods. Another change is that you will add one green juice and one smoothie a day. Use the smoothie recipes and green juice recipes in the next chapter to make delicious meals and snacks. There are also many smoothie recipes available online. Try to stick to one or two fruits in each smoothie, so there are not too many fruits at once. I like to use bananas as the base and then add one fruit and a leafy green; you can throw in a date if you like it sweeter. Dates are so incredibly healing and nutritious. They are a perfect sweetener if you have a sweet tooth.

- Note if you are struggling with severe Acne I suggest doing the celery juice in the morning and waiting atleast 45 min before any fruit. The mineral salts in the celery juice will start to kill off the bacteria, and pathogens that could be causing your breakouts!

Week Two: Days 8–14

Things get a little more disciplined this week. Last week, we only eliminated foods and added smoothies and green juices. This week, we will add supplements and restrict foods after certain times, all while keeping the first week's guidelines. Again, you will not feel deprived or hungry if you eat enough of the living food, which will help to restore your skin's health. You will eat nothing but fruit and leafy greens until lunchtime. This actually makes life so simple—talk about fast food. You can have a whole watermelon or a cantaloupe for breakfast, two mangoes, a huge fruit smoothie (my suggestion), or a fruit bowl. There are so many amazing fruits in the world, and we have the luxury of eating a wide array of them. Get creative, and enjoy all the delicious, hydrating fruits that nature has to offer, from the time you wake up until lunchtime. Stop eating any fruit for sixty minutes before you eat lunch. You want to make sure you are not mixing foods.

Below are the week-two guidelines for the 7-7-7 total skin detox. Depending on how toxic your liver is, you may feel great at this point, or you may start to release lots of pathogens and feel a bit like you have the flu. It takes about seven to ten days for alcohol, medications, and other chemical substances to clear out of the system, so be patient if you don't feel so great. Some medications or drugs can take months to clear out of the system. You will get there. Try to not take any over-the-counter medications while doing this. If you are on prescriptions, it is up to you and your doctor to decide if getting off them and healing with nutrition, supplements, and food may be a better option for you. In my opinion, there are very few illnesses that living foods can't reverse.

Breakfast

Lemon water
Only fruit until noon or your lunchtime every day for the next seven days.
You can do a fruit bowl, grab loose fruit, have smoothies, or however you fancy your fruit. Leafy greens are ok.

Lunch/Dinner

You can enjoy any veggies and any legumes you want, as long as you do well with them. Raw is best, but if you can't do raw, you can steam or roast your veggies—preferably steam if you have to cook them because it keeps the veggies hydrated, which keeps you hydrated. You can also enjoy gluten-free bread, as long as it's organic and non-GMO and has no sugar or dairy. Watch out for the bad oils in any of the gluten-free breads or wraps. Wraps are a great way to roll up a bunch of fresh veggies and enjoy. You also can make a delicious dipping sauce. I've included my favorite vegan dips that you can use to spice up your life. Potatoes are also a staple on this cleanse. Potatoes are very healing and can give you the sustenance you need to sustain on a cleanse like this. Potatoes are not bad for you. They are full of minerals and nutrients that can help you heal. You will not gain weight from eating potatoes, if you do this cleanse properly. (See recipes for lunch/dinner ideas.)

Supplements to Add

Adding your supplements to your smoothies is a great way to get them down. I break open the capsules and blend in my supplements. Taking them by mouth is also just as good. If you find it hard to swallow capsules, the smoothie option would be best.

Vitamin C	3000 mg, twice a day
Lysine	2000 mg twice a day
Zinc (liquid zinc sulfate)	recommended dose
Spirulina	1 teaspoon
Vegan DHA/EPA	recommended dose

Snack ideas: Smoothies, Dates, hummus, veggie sticks, cherry tomatoes,

Rules to Remember

No fat whatsoever before noon—not even good fats, like avocado, nuts, vegan cheese, or butter. If you mess up, just pick up where you left off—it's OK. Keep the fat intake to under 15 grams a day, and that can come from plants or nuts only. You are giving your liver a break from all the fat for a short time so it has a break to clean out. Any fat slows down cleansing. Period.

No food after 8:00 p.m.—only lemon water, herbal tea, or coconut waters. Do not mix your fruits with any other foods, but you can mix leafy greens and fruits. Do not mix your vegetables and fruit.

Week Two Background

In this second week, we are creating a program in which you do not eat anything but fruit and hydration for sixteen hours. From 8:00 p.m. until noon the next day, you have only water, tea, and fruit—but all you want of it. Take advantage of the vast array of choices. You are not technically intermittently fasting because you are eating the fruit, but in a sense, you are fasting on fruit. Fruits digest quickly and allow your body to use the antiviral properties and repairing nutrients to help clean out and let the detox organs do the work they are meant to do, which is to clean up the body. It's very likely your detox organs are overloaded. When we fast, we clean out, but we are not giving the body any fuel to help it sustain itself, so you can get weak and tired when you cleanse. It's like washing the dishes without soap. Fruit enzymes actually eat up and break down all the bad stuff. Cleansing with fruit is safe and will keep you sustained through the cleansing process.

One of the best things from this plan is that you might notice how much energy you have and how happy and alive you feel from all the living high-vibrational food you are taking in. Your liver starts to release the bad things, so it's very important that you continue this plan until the end. You do not want it to start to release and then stop, as it will absorb it all back up again. It's truly amazing once you reach this stage of the process. Hang in there when you feel like you don't want to continue. The more toxic you are, the longer it will take. You are letting go of old stuff, and it's not always easy. Your body is used to a certain way, and now you are changing that way.

Week Three

This week is split in two, and it gets a bit disciplined.

Days 15–18: Only Smoothies and Green Juices

This is when things start really changing. For three solid days, you will be on a liquid diet of green juice, smoothies, raw soups, water, and herbal tea. It's only three days—you can do this! You will feel incredible from it, and your skin should start to glow, unless you are super-toxic; then you might still have purges in your skin, like breakouts or rashes. These things will clear up if you keep pushing forward. It's a process, so if your skin looks worse or you're having breakouts, don't worry; it's not failing. It's working! It's changing. There are some great recipes and meal ideas in the next chapter so get creative! Make sure you get enough food in these three days. Don't skip any meals, and if you feel hungry, have another smoothie, make a juice, or blend up another soup. Do not suffer or feel hungry during these three days. You're using the blender as a second stomach to make digestion easier and give your system a break so it can work on cleaning you up.

Day 19-21: Back to the First-Week Plan

This means you can eat solid foods again but don't eat anything from the no-no list. Keep adding the smoothies and green juice. Start adding solid foods back in slowly so you do not overwhelm your system.

After day 21, you can start over, and do the twenty-one days again for as long as you want. If you decide to add any of the no-nos back into the diet, try to eat only *non-GMO* versions of corn, soy, and dairy. They are not good for you or your skin, but realistically, I know that many people are not ready to give up a taco or chips and salsa or their other favorite no-nos. Just remember that there are many substitutes for corn chips and tortillas and breads that use cassava, rice, and chickpea flours. Corn, dairy, soy, toxic oils, and eggs all feed the bugs and viruses inside of us. The more food these bugs have, the bigger they get. We want to eat a diet that is antiviral and plant-based because we live in a very contaminated world at this time. We need to give our bodies the strength they need to survive and thrive. We can't ask for things to get easier right now, so we need to ask for more strength. Living foods give us that strength and vitality to help our bodies stay strong in very uncertain times here on earth. Choose living foods, and you will choose life, health, and beauty!

After the twenty-one days, people say that they have relief from aches and pains, skin rashes, and moodiness. They can sleep better, they look brighter and fresher, and their bowel movements are normal again. So many positive results come from a living-food diet. This is a twenty-one-day challenge that you can repeat safely, over and over again. It's a way of life, not a diet.

CHAPTER 19

Skin Food Recipes: Juices and Smoothies for Glowing Skin

Organic Produce

Please only buy and use organic produce! Organic produce actually has more nutrients than conventionally grown produce. You can feel safe that you are not ingesting more toxins, like pesticides and chemicals that hurt your health as well as your looks. Also, the conditions in which organic produce is grown contribute to a natural growing process that allows the plants to produce more of the antioxidants and nutrients that our bodies need to fight off aging and disease. Many will say that this is not true, but many studies have shown otherwise. You may have to dig deep for the truth on this one. Also, eating organically helps promote the proper farming that produces healthy food, instead of supporting the GMO food culture. Be a part of the cure, not the disease.

Organic green juices and smoothies are a great way to pack in the nutrients. They are fast and so delicious.

If you drink two smoothies and two green juices a day, your skin will change fast. This is a great way to prepare for an event or a wedding. You will get the glow.

The Brilliant-Skin Smoothie

5 kale leaves
1 cup frozen pineapple
1/2 cup clean water or coconut water

Optional: Coconut milk is a great addition to this.
Instead of 3/4 cup clean water, try 1/4 cup clean water and 1/2 cup of coconut milk.
If you have skin issues like rashes, though, I would stick with water or coconut water. The coconut milk may have too much fat for the liver to process if it's dealing with other pathogens. A little coconut milk is OK, but try to limit your intake of fat (good and bad) when dealing with skin disorders. We need the liver to start functioning at a high level again, and too much fat just clogs it up.

Radiant-Skin Juice

(Hydrating and anti-inflammatory)
1 cucumber
1 head of kale
1 lemon
2 apples
Optional: ginger

Skin-Flush Green Juice

1 lemon
1 large bunch of spinach
2–3 green apples

Liver-Cleanse Juice

16–32 ounces of celery juice (do not add anything else)

Celery works as a medicinal herb and is one of the most detoxifying herbs you can drink to heal your body from illness. It's not a fad; it's a miracle juice, and it works. The mineral salts in celery help to restore your digestive health and help to detox the body. It can help digestion problems fast. If you have skin rashes, I strongly recommend drinking straight celery juice every morning. Drink 16–32 ounce; then you can have a different juice later in the day. Do not add lemon or anything else to the celery juice. Do this every day if you are dealing with rosacea, acne, psoriasis, or eczema. This juice is the most important juice for you. Drink it at least once a day; twice a day, if possible.

Smoothie Meal Replacement

2 bananas (frozen are OK)
2 dates
1 cup frozen wild blueberries
big handful of spinach
1 scoop of spirulina (Hawaiian)
coconut water or regular spring water

Blend to desired thickness; then add supplements.

If you don't like the taste of the spirulina in a smoothie, find another way to get this into your diet. Try capsules if the powder is too strong of a taste. Spirulina is the most nutrient-dense food on the planet.

Basil-Cell–Repair Smoothie

2 bananas
1 cup of frozen pineapple
1/2 cup of basil
2 dates
water or coconut water to desired thickness (coconut water preferred)

Pimple-Popper Smoothie (for Acne)

2 bananas (frozen are OK)
1 cup of frozen organic cherries (antiviral, antibacterial)
juice of 1/2 lemon

1 handful of spinach
water or coconut water for desired thickness.
vitamin C
zinc sulphate (1 dropper)

The Skin-Plump Green Smoothie

1 banana
1 cup spinach
1/2 avocado
5 kale leaves
2 dates
1/4 cup clean water (or coconut water)

Spicy Mango Soup (in the blender)

1 large mango
1/2 cup clean water
1 small chili pepper
1 teaspoon ginger
squeeze of lime

Raw Cream of Broccoli (in the blender)

4 cups of broccoli
1.5 cups water
pinch of salt
1/2 cup raw cashews
1/2 cup chopped celery
1/4 cup onion
1 teaspoon dill
2 tablespoons coconut amino
1 teaspoon rosemary

Other Meal Ideas for the 7-7-7 Total Skin Detox

Steamed potatoes (potatoes are very nutritious and healing; they are not too many carbs! Enjoy them.) Potatoes are one of the most nutritious foods you can eat.

Baked potatoes

Roasted cauliflower

Brussels sprouts

Steamed or roasted asparagus

Chopped salads

Vegan dishes that follow the guidelines.

Just watch out for those bad oils.

I recommend any of Anthony William's books for recipes and cleansing ideas. He is the original celery-juice promoter. As I mentioned earlier in the book, his information is life-changing.

Should I Buy a Juicer or a Blender?

If you are going to be juicing, I strongly recommend investing in a good juicer. Green juices are not cheap, and you'll want to get those juices in every day to get the beautiful glow you are trying to achieve.

I suggest a cold-press juicer. The slow mastication of the extraction ensures you do not heat up the enzymes and kill them before they are consumed. The high-nutrient content of the juice helps heal the skin and cleanse the body.

A Vitamix or a Bullet is great too, and I am all for them, but each is considered more of a smoothie blender. I like the cold press because you can get more nutrients from one juice because of the number of veggies and fruits it takes to get one juice.

The fiber is not in the juice, and processing it is one less function your body has to perform. It allows your organs to take a break and just absorb the powerful nutrients. The fiber is what you poop out, so you can let the juicer do this step for you, especially if you are healing from a skin disorder.

However, I love the idea of having the fiber and whole vegetable blended, and I encourage that in addition to the pure juice. If you do not have access to this method, then, by all means, juice or blend it however you can. A Vitamix is amazing for making soups and smoothies.

Smoothies are a great way to pack in the vitamins, and you can make an amazing meal from a smoothie—talk about fast food! Throw in a banana, a handful of spinach, a date, some frozen blueberries, some spirulina powder—and you just made a delicious meal that will feed your skin, your brain, and your soul with living high-vibrational food. No mess, no stress, and kids absolutely love smoothies—a bonus if you are a busy mom.

Smoothies are such a good way to sneak in the stuff that kids need so desperately to be healthy in this modern world. Doing both smoothies and cold-pressed juices is great.

CHAPTER 20

Conscious Living

What Is Conscious Living?

Conscious living is becoming aware of your actions and how they affect your environment, your planet, animals, others—and yourself.

If you are new to the idea of knowing where your food comes from or where your products are being made and what is in them, it can seem like a lot of work and just too mind-boggling. I promise you, it's not! It can seem a bit overwhelming when you first start, but after a while, you may realize that it's simple. It's like taking ten steps back to move one hundred steps forward. After you have done the work of finding out what is safe to use and who you choose to support in the world, you can rest, knowing you are making choices that are safe. I have my go-to products, foods, and cleaners that I know I can trust. If something new comes out, I do the research and approve it. You do need to be careful, however, if a trusted company is bought up by someone, and they change the standards or ingredients. It happens often, so be aware.

I love this explanation of becoming conscious: *there is an I, and a self, and the I becomes the observer of the self.* When we observe ourselves and our actions, we can become more aware of our connection to everything. We are not just on autopilot anymore. If we wake up and start making better choices in our own lives, it makes a difference beyond just ourselves. Conscious living is simply being awake and choosing things that better our lives and the lives of others.

The Power of Thinking and Skin

I once heard a famous celebrity say that she talked to her cells in her body and that staying positive was one of her biggest beauty secrets! I absolutely loved this attitude and her vigor for life. That glow that she has comes from inside. Your glow comes from how you feel, how you look at the world, and how you look at yourself. Waking up each morning, looking in the mirror, and seeing the beauty inside you—not the flaws—will truly help you stay young.

Your emotions and feelings are a way that your brain registers information about your body. If you are constantly negative about yourself, I believe you will manifest rapid aging. Meet yourself where you are right now, in the present moment. Pick an age (realistically) that you want to look and feel, and believe that you already do! You'll be surprised how the belief itself will become the actual feeling of being healthy and beautiful. It will give you an inner glow that people will notice. Just a smile can take off ten years.

Imagining your skin and health in a perfect state can have a huge impact. The power of visualization is incredible. Your thoughts are always moving you in one direction or the other. Why not choose the direction you want to go? You have a lot more power over your thoughts and how you see yourself than you may think. "Fake it until you make it" is a great saying. When you act as if you already have that which you desire, your brain starts believing, and you naturally move towards your desire. Hold yourself in the highest vibration of love and compassion and already see the skin you desire. The Bible says to pray as if it is already done. I believe in this tremendously.

> Truly I tell you that if anyone says to this mountain, 'Be lifted up and thrown into the sea,' and has no doubt in his heart but believes that it will happen, it will be done for him. Therefore I tell you, whatever you ask in prayer, believe that you have received it, and it will be yours.
> —Mark 11:23–25

"Every Time I Start Something, It Only Lasts for
a Few Days. How Do I Make It Stick?"

Clients ask me all the time, "When should I start changing my habits?"
or "When should I schedule a skin detox?"

These are such important questions. If we hate something and feel like
we are suffering, our brains will trick us into giving up and writing off the
experience as a flop. Here's my advice on when to start a habit change or
skin detox, how to stay with it, and how to enjoy it all the while.

Pick a date. Make a three-week commitment.

This way, you prepare the subconscious for an adventure. Your brain
has a way of sticking to something better if it is prepared. If you are
preparing for a wedding or a high school reunion, you can pick a date a
month before the event. You potentially could pick a date three months
ahead, and do the plan twice before the event. You could repeat the twenty-
one days over and over again. It will only benefit your skin.

The good thing about a skin detox is that you get to eat lots of delicious
fruits and veggies. You should never feel deprived or unsatisfied. When I
know that I have not been on track as well as I could be, I usually pick a
date a week in advance. I will hold the date in my mind and go all-in on
the morning of the desired date.

Remember that lots of brands and companies want you to buy their
products. See through the veil of marketing for what it is. Companies will
go to great lengths to sell you something. Stick with companies that are
honest, small, transparent, organic, and cruelty-free. When you tap into
this world and see the truth of things, it makes it much easier to *want* to
eat fewer animals, use fewer chemicals, buy safe foods and skin products,
and fill your body and mind with the truth.

We think of something bigger than ourselves when we become
conscious of this stuff. The cool thing is that we all benefit from the
changes each of us makes.

If you have this knowledge before you start the changes, it makes it
exciting to be part of a movement to lift the vibration of the planet, starting
with your own body.

When I was young, I used to think that we were little cells inside a
big body, and that big body was a cell inside another big body. Now that

I am an adult and understand more about the earth, I think I wasn't that far off. Think of yourself as a living cell in the body of the planet. Are you a healthy cell or a sick cell? Are you part of the cure or part of the disease?

Willpower

Whenever we want to change a habit or start or stop something in our lives, we rely on our willpower. This can be really tricky. For some people, this creates an internal war in their minds that can be quite draining and cause them to write off the whole idea. Imagine being in a fight with someone all the time, except the someone is you!

What if you did not have to rely on willpower and, instead, you counted on your belief system? When you change a belief system to align with your actions, you no longer have the *desire* to do that which you were trying to stop doing. This is because your brain doesn't actually *believe* that the action you are trying to stop will make you feel good anymore. This is the reason why learning how things affect you negatively is a good way to stop a bad habit.

Your Glow Is Contagious

We may not realize the cause and effect of our actions. With family, friends, strangers, and, most importantly, our children, everything we do is an example. When we look healthy and glowing, it's almost contagious. When you start shining and feeling amazing, people will notice and want to know your secrets.

An example of this is when I started eating super-healthy and buying mostly living foods at my local grocery store. Since I live in a small community, the grocery clerks now take notice. Every time I go into the store and line up all my fresh fruit and vegetables on the conveyor belt, people ask questions. Imagine a cart full of only fruits and veggies. It always starts a healthy conversation about food.

People are shocked to see sixty bananas and twenty oranges in my cart—and then I'm back the next week to get more. They can see that my kids are happy and glowing, and they start to think that maybe there *is* something to this fruit-and-veggie thing!

I then have an opportunity to (hopefully) give at least one person a health tip that may very well change his or her life for the better (but only if they ask or they are interested—I try not to be annoying).

When my kids see me juicing and eating well, they want to do the same. When my friends see my skin glowing, they want to know which fountain of youth I'm drinking from. It's contagious. When Gandhi said, "Be the change you want to see," this is what he meant. When Jesus said, "Your body is the temple of God," this is what he meant.

I used to have incredible guilt that doing good for myself was selfish, and I would put myself last on the list. It actually ended up creating the opposite effect in my life than what I thought I was creating. I got worn out, moody, resentful, and overwhelmed that I was falling behind in my duties. It wasn't until I started taking care of myself—nurturing my mind and body with rest, good food, exercise, and time for myself—that I actually became much more productive. I was able to give others so much more when I actually took time for myself.

I now feel guilty if I neglect myself because I know it's then that I will be useless to those who need me. Now the time I spend working is focused and meaningful, and I feel so much more satisfied.

You deserve to have beautiful skin, and you deserve to know the truth about why your skin is suffering. You deserve to be happy when you look in the mirror. We *all* have the gift of beauty waiting inside us. With living food and a high-vibrational lifestyle, you can unleash the beauty within and live a life well lived.

With love,
Amy Rae

ABOUT THE AUTHOR

Amy Rae has been in the beauty, aesthetics, and medical aesthetic industry for close to twenty years. She is a licensed aesthetician in the states of California and Florida. She also has a holistic practitioner certification. Her unique approach of combining nutritional skin care with a holistic topical approach has made her one of Southern California's most sought-after aestheticians. Amy Rae has been featured on shows such as *Botched* and *WAGS* on the E! Entertainment channel. She has also been written up in many beauty magazines such as ELLE and allure magazine. Her Beverly Boulevard location was named one of the "Top 10 Spas in Los Angeles" by *The LAist*. The spa was also featured on *The Chalk Board*, Refinery29 and the *Los Angeles Times* and other top publications in Los Angeles. Many celebrities trust Amy Rae with their skin and have for years. Amy Rae uses skin nutrition to help target the root cause of problematic skin issues.

After retiring from physically working on clients in her private spas in West Hollywood and Pacific Palisades, California, to spend time with her husband and four daughters, Amy Rae decided to write this book in hopes of sharing her skin care secrets. Amy Rae's unconventional approach works for the long-term health and beauty of the skin, and it has inspired thousands of people to trust her with their skin over the years. It is her passion to help those who have been struggling with problematic skin issues to finally find answers and get to the root cause of the issues.

Printed in the United States
by Baker & Taylor Publisher Services